Innovative Congressional
Minimum Standards
Preemption Statutes

Innovative Congressional Minimum Standards Preemption Statutes

JOSEPH F. ZIMMERMAN

SUNY
PRESS

Published by
STATE UNIVERSITY OF NEW YORK PRESS, ALBANY

© 2016 State University of New York

All rights reserved

Printed in the United States of America

For information, contact
State University of New York Press, Albany, NY
www.sunypress.edu

Production, Laurie D. Searl
Marketing, Michael Campochiaro

Library of Congress Cataloging-in-Publication Data

Names: Zimmerman, Joseph Francis, 1928– author.
Title: Innovative Congressional minimum standards preemption statutes /
    Joseph F. Zimmerman.
Description: Albany : State University of New York Press, 2016. | Includes
    bibliographical references and index.
Identifiers: LCCN 2015026351| ISBN 9781438460970 (hardcover : alk. paper) |
    ISBN 9781438460987 (paperback : alk. paper) | 9781438460994 (e-book)
Subjects: LCSH: Exclusive and concurrent legislative powers—United States. |
    Environmental law—United States.
Classification: LCC KF4600.Z565 2016 | DDC 342.73/042—dc23
LC record available at http://lccn.loc.gov/2015026351

10   9   8   7   6   5   4   3   2   1

To Dahl Taylor, with many thanks!

Contents

Preface   ix

Chapter 1   The Nature of Preemption   1

Chapter 2   Minimum National Water-Quality and
Drinking-Water Standards Preemption   29

Chapter 3   Minimum National Air-Quality Standards
Preemption   53

Chapter 4   Maximum State Regulatory Standards and
Regulatory Authority Turn-Back Statutes   67

Chapter 5   State-Friendly Preemption Statutes   77

Chapter 6   Contingent Preemption Statutes   83

Chapter 7   Innovative Congressional Preemption Statutes:
An Evaluation   101

Notes   113

Bibliography   131

Index   147

Preface

Congress enacted the first two complete preemption statutes (Copy Right Act and Patent Act) in 1790 that removed subnational governmental regulatory powers in these two areas. Congress subsequently enacted preemption acts at a slow pace, and only twenty-nine preemption acts were enacted by the turn of the twentieth century. The pace of congressional enactment of preemption statutes remained slow until the pace increased, dramatically commencing in the 1960s. By 2015, a total of 704 preemption acts had been enacted with or without the support of a relatively large number of interests groups. A preemption act may contain a sunset clause establishing a specific date for the termination of the act. Subnational government leaders often criticize preemption acts, particularly ones containing mandates and/or restraints, and on occasion urge Congress to enact a preemption act because states have been unable to solve a public problem by means of cooperative interstate action. In addition, the entry of the United States into treaties with foreign nations may preempt certain regulatory powers of states completely or partially.

These acts have produced major changes in the nature of the federal system as Congress employed its preemption powers to remove regulatory authority completely, partially, or contingently from state governments and local governments. The framers of the U.S. Constitution designed the new governmental system to allow Congress to respond to changing conditions by delegating to it latent powers. The metamorphic system remains an *imperium in imperio*, with state governments continuing to exercise important regulatory powers. The system has not been converted into a unitary system; even more regulatory fields are the exclusive responsibility of Congress.

Preemption acts until 1965 were either complete preemption acts removing all regulatory powers from state and local governments or partial preemption acts occupying only part of a regulatory field. The

Water Quality Act of 1965 is an innovative partial preemption act establishing minimum water quality standards, and authorizing each state to continue to regulate, provided the state adopts standards equal to or more stringent than the federal standards. A second innovative partial preemption statute is the contingent Voting Rights Act of 1965, providing that it applies to a state only if two conditions prevail in the state.

The reader should be aware Congress on occasion devolves one of its delegated powers to the states, and has done so since 1789, when states were authorized to regulate marine port pilots. The most important devolution statute is the McCarran-Ferguson Act of 1945, devolving regulatory authority to the states to regulate the insurance industry. This volume examines congressional turn-backs of authority to state attorneys generals and state-friendly congressional preemption statutes.

The pace of enactment of preemption acts has slowed dramatically since the Republican Party captured control of the U.S. House of Representatives in the 2010 general elections, while the Democrats controlled the presidency and the Senate. In all probability, Congress in the future will enact preemption statutes at a faster pace to cope with domestic and foreign problems.

A special debt of gratitude is owed to Barbara Mathews for her assistance in gathering data and information for inclusion in this volume.

Chapter 1

The Nature of Preemption

This volume builds upon my 2005 book titled *Congressional Preemption: Regulatory Federalism*, which presents a broad overview of congressional use of preemption powers since 1790 to remove completely or partially state regulatory powers in various fields such as bankruptcy, civil rights, gun control, occupational safety, and water quality.[1] The book notes Congress, commencing in 1965, enacted the first of a new type of preemption statute that I label an innovative preemption statute. The book also briefly reviews this new preemption type in contrast to this book that is devoted primarily to various types of innovative preemption statutes and their relative success in achieving congressionally established goals. A review of constitutional developments will facilitate an understanding of the importance of innovative preemption statutes.

The U.S. Constitution established the world's first federal system in 1789, an *Imperium in Imperio* (an empire within an empire), by dividing exercisable powers between the newly established general government and the thirteen state governments. The fundamental law delegates specific powers to Congress and other specific powers to the president, reserves all other powers with the exceptions of prohibited ones to the states, and allows states to exercise other specified powers with the consent of Congress. The powers delegated to Congress by the U.S. Constitution are latent ones that may be employed at will. The drafters of the fundamental law recognized the undesirability of a static distribution of political powers between the national government and the states, and included provisions for the amendment of the fundamental law and other provisions authorizing Congress to enact statutes removing

1

completely or partially or contingently specific regulatory powers from the state governments.

The reserved powers include the English common law and equity that states continue to employ subsequent to the issuance of the Declaration of Independence in 1776. A most important component of the common law is the police power that is definable only in the broadest terms as the power of states to regulate persons and properties in order to protect and promote public health, safety, welfare, morals, and convenience. State and local governments were the principal regulators until well into the twentieth century, when Congress became a most important regulator and employed more frequently its constitutionally granted broad powers to remove completely or partially or contingently regulatory powers from states and by extension from local governments. The reader should note that not all preemption statutes contain an explicit preemption clause, and courts are called upon to determine whether a statute is preemptive.

Congress possessed the power to preempt completely certain concurrent state powers since 1789, but the power was not exercised after the enactment in 1790 of the Copyright Act and the Patent Act until 1946 when the Atomic Energy Act was enacted.[2] Several complete preemption statutes—atomic energy, grain standards, and railroad safety are examples—have been amended by Congress to allow states to play a role in the administration of these statutes.[3]

Congressional exercise of its preemption powers in an innovative manner since 1965 produced major changes in the nature of the federal system without a constitutional amendment.

Congress, commencing with the Voting Rights Act of 1965, enacted innovative preemption statutes differing significantly from the earlier preemption statutes.[4] We classify these statutes as minimum national standards preemption, contingent preemption, maximum national standards preemption, regulatory authority turn-backs, and state-friendly preemption statutes.

Two theories explaining the federal system in the United States are well known. The theory of dual federalism, a legalistic one, posits there is a constitutional division of exercisable powers between the national government and the state governments.[5] James Madison in effect was the author of theory of cooperative federalism that gained prominence after World War II, and emphasizes the cooperation between the three planes of government: national, state, and local.[6]

A brief review of the events leading to the drafting and ratification of the U.S. Constitution, and a listing of its key provisions will facilitate an understanding of the congressional development of congressional minimum standards and other innovative preemption statutes pertaining to water quality, air quality, drinking-water quality, surface mining, insecticides, fungicides, and rodenticides. These relatively new innovative statutes supplement the complete preemption acts, removing all regulatory powers from states in a given field since 1790. Each state is authorized to continue regulating in each of the above five fields, provided the state has standards at least as stringent as the federal standards, qualified personnel, and the necessary equipment.

CONSTITUTIONAL DEVELOPMENTS

The Declaration of Independence in 1776 officially dissolved the ties of each of the thirteen former colonies to the United Kingdom, and established them as nation-states that entered into a loose military alliance. The superintendence of the prosecution of the successful Revolutionary War was the responsibility of the Second Continental Congress, a unicameral body composed of an equal number of members from each state. The thirteen states and the United Kingdom signed the Treaty of Paris of 1783, granting independence to the states.

ARTICLES OF CONFEDERATION

The Congress that prosecuted the Revolutionary War recognized the need for a more permanent structure of government, and in 1777 proposed the Articles of Confederation and Perpetual Union providing for a league of amity. Boundary disputes, however, delayed ratification until 1781, when the thirteenth state, Maryland, ratified the articles.

The most important provision was Article II, which declared, "Each State retains its sovereignty, freedom and independence, and every power, jurisdiction and right, which is not by this confederation expressly delegated to the united States in Congress assembled." The drafters employed a lowercase *u* in united to emphasize a national government had not been established, and the articles were a treaty uniting the states for only expressed purposes.

Article III explained the new government was "a firm league of friendship," and described its purposes as "common defense, the security of their liberties, and their mutual and general welfare, binding themselves to assist each other, against all force offered to, or attacks made upon them, or by any of them, on account of religion, sovereignty, trade, or other pretense whatever."

Three important provisions promoting harmonious interstate relations were incorporated in Article IV: Citizens of a state as sojourners in sister states were entitled to the privileges and immunities of citizens in each state visited; the governor of the asylum state must return fugitives from justice to the requesting state; and each state must give full faith and credit to the legislative acts, records, and final judicial proceedings of courts in the other states. These provisions are incorporated in Article IV of the U.S. Constitution, as they are essential for the health of a confederacy or a federal union.

Each state legislature was authorized by Article V to appoint two to seven delegates to the unicameral Congress subject to recall. A three-year term limit over a six-year period was established for delegates appointed annually in a manner determined by each state legislature. A state's delegates collectively possessed a single vote. The reader should note the articles importantly did not establish an executive branch or a judicial branch.

The Congress was granted few powers: borrow and coin money, declare war, establish a postal system and standards of weights and measures, negotiate treaties with foreign nations, regulate relations with Indian tribes, and set a quota for each state to furnish men and funds for the army. The limited powers of the Congress and the lack of authority to levy taxes predestined the confederacy to failure.

DEFECTS

The defects of the articles and the weakness of the Congress quickly were revealed by experience. Specific defects included Congress's reliance upon voluntary state contributions of funds, lack of authority to regulate interstate commerce and enforce its laws, difficulty in obtaining funds from foreign lenders, and inability to suppress disorders within states.

The printing of paper money was authorized by Congress, but such money almost immediately became worthless because of the lack of authority to levy taxes to raise revenue. This problem was not the only serious one. Article VI forbade states to "lay any imposts or duties which may interfere with stipulations in treaties" entered into by Congress with foreign nations, but Article IX stipulated commerce treaties may not prevent a state "from prohibiting the exportation or importation of any species of goods or commodities whatsoever . . ." Furthermore, the articles did not prohibit state-erected interstate trade barriers that soon brought interstate commerce to a near standstill.[7]

The end of the confederation was hastened by Captain Daniel Shays who served in the army during the Revolutionary War, and subsequently lead a rebellion of disgruntled farmers in western Massachusetts in 1786, which spread to within forty-five miles of Boston. They sought a lowering of real property taxes, cheap money, and suspension of mortgage foreclosures. The Commonwealth of Massachusetts was powerless to suppress the rebellion, and it was suppressed only when wealthy Boston residents raised funds for an army led by General Benjamin Lincoln.[8]

The articles' serious defects persuaded the Maryland and the Virginia boundary commissioners in 1785 to recommend the sending of delegates by each state to a meeting in Annapolis in 1786 to develop remedies. Only five states sent delegates who memorialized Congress to call a convention to consider drafting amendments to the articles. Congress responded by calling a convention to meet in Philadelphia in 1787.

THE CONSTITUTIONAL CONVENTION

Only Rhode Island failed to send delegates to the convention that met from March 25 to September 17, 1787. States appointed seventy-four delegates, but nineteen refused to accept appointments or did not attend the convention. The convention was divided by philosophical and sectional differences with delegates representing the former expressing the fear a stronger national government would be a threat to individual liberties. The sectional differences were based on the nature of the economy in each region. Five days of negotiations led to a six-to-one decision to replace the Articles of Confederation and Perpetual Union with a new constitution. Delegates from five states had not arrived by the time of the vote.

Delegates debated whether the proposed Congress should be granted authority to review and invalidate state laws before they would become effective, but decided the constitution should not delegate this power. A major controversy concerned state representation in the proposed unicameral Congress with states with small populations pressing for equal representation for each state as under the Articles of Confederation. The Connecticut compromise resolved this controversy by providing for a bicameral national legislature with a Senate representing each state equally and a House representing each state in accordance with its population, with the proviso that each state would have a minimum of one representative.

The third controversy involved slavery, with the northern states generally advocating the immediate termination of the importation of slaves. Delegates approved a compromise clause providing slaves could be imported for twenty years and Congress could levy a tax of up to ten dollars on each imported slave.

The fourth controversy involved whether Congress should be authorized to impose import duties and export duties. The northern states favored both duties as sources of national revenue, and the southern states opposed the duties because they would be paying most of the duties in view of the facts they exported the bulk of their products, which were chiefly agricultural, and imported most of their needed manufactured products. The compromise provided that Congress could tax imports but not exports.

There was no serious opposition to fifteen of the eighteen powers proposed to be delegated to Congress. Furthermore, there was near unanimous agreement regarding the various prohibitions placed upon Congress and the requirement states must obtain congressional permission to initiate specified proposed actions, including entrance into interstate compacts or agreements, or levying of imposts on imports and exports.

The proposed constitution in Section 10 of Article I contains preemption provisions removing powers from the states. "No state shall enter in any treaty, alliance or confederation; grant letters of marque and reprisal; coin money; emit bills of credit; make anything but gold and silver coin a tender in payment of debts; pass any bill of attainder, *ex post facto* law, or law impairing the obligation of contracts, or grant any title of nobility."

The Constitution authorizes two types of concurrent powers. The first type includes the power of states to levy taxes immune from formal congressional preemption or court invalidation, unless they impose a burden on interstate commerce or violate the privileges and immunities clause or equal protection of the law clause of the Constitution. The second type includes powers expressly delegated to Congress and not prohibited to states, as illustrated by regulation of interstate commerce. The existence of concurrent powers can result in clashes between a congressional statute and a state statute. The drafters of the Constitution were aware such potential conflicts would occur and incorporated the supremacy of the law clause in Article VI, providing for the prevalence of the congressional statute wherever there is a conflict. This type of concurrent power exercised by a state legislature is subject to complete or partial preemption by a congressional statute.

Section 10 of Article I also permits state legislatures to exercise certain otherwise prohibited powers with the consent of Congress— levying of import and tonnage duties, keeping troops in time of peace, and entering into compacts or agreements with sister states. The reader should note the U.S. Supreme Court has not always opined these powers can be exercised only with congressional consent. In 1893, the court in

Virginia v. Tennessee noted such approval is required only if two or more states desire to enter into "political compacts" affecting the balance of powers between the general government and the states.[9] The court in 1975 opined the prohibition of levying "imposts or duties on imports" without the consent of Congress does not prevent imposition of an *ad valorem* property tax on imported tires.[10] The court issued a generally similar ruling in 1986, upholding the authority of Durham County, North Carolina, to impose an *ad valorem* property tax on imported tobacco stored in customs-bonded storehouses for future incorporation in domestic manufacturing on the grounds the tax did not violate the import-export clause of the U.S. Constitution, and was not preempted by an act of Congress.[11]

The reader should note citizens residing within states receive all of their public services, except the postal service, from state governments and/or local governments. Congress, of course, influences the provision of many of these services by offering conditional grants-in-aid to subnational governments. Acceptance by a state government or a local government of one of these grants binds the recipient unit to abide by the attached conditions. Congress may authorize the provision of many services on federal properties located within states, such as education for children of military personnel.

The proposed constitution would establish a strong president, a Supreme Court, and a Congress possessing specific delegated powers (see below). Fear of a centralized government was reduced by inclusion of "checks and balances" designed to protect the semi-sovereignty of the states and individual liberties from abuse.

RATIFICATION CAMPAIGN

The proposed constitution, which was not a popular document, was sent by the convention to the thirteen state legislatures with the proviso each should arrange for the election of delegates to a special convention with the power to ratify or to reject the document. Several objections immediately were raised: the convention was called to revise the Articles of Confederation and Perpetual Union and not to discard them, the articles could be amended only with the unanimous consent of the states, the proposed Congress either would be too strong or too weak, and the new government either would be too independent of the states or too dependent upon them. The strongest opposition was in the interior of the nation and regions with a small population. Farmers and imprisoned debtors not surprisingly favored cheap paper money issued by states.

The proposed constitution forbade Congress to suspend the writ of habeas corpus unless a rebellion or an invasion threatens public safety. Congress and the states were forbidden to enact a bill of attainder or an ex post facto law, and to impair the obligation of contracts. Many of the opponents' criticisms centered on the lack of a bill of rights, similar to the rights in state constitutions guaranteeing freedom of assembly, petition, press, religion, and speech. Proponents of the draft constitution argued a bill of rights would be superfluous in view of the fact the proposed fundamental law does not grants powers to Congress to abridge the liberties of citizens.

Article VII of the proposed constitution provided it would become effective upon ratification by nine states. The proposed fundamental law was ratified quickly by the Delaware, New Jersey, and Pennsylvania conventions, and their approvals were followed by the approval of conventions in Connecticut and Georgia. Strong opposition continued in Massachusetts, New York, and Virginia, and their rejection would doom the proposed constitution.

THE FEDERALIST AND ANTIFEDERALIST PAPERS

Alexander Hamilton, John Jay, and James Madison wrote a series of eighty-five letters to editors of New York City newspapers during the winter and spring of 1787 to 1788 to convince delegates to the state convention to ratify the proposed constitution. Thirty-six letters were published as a book in late March 1788, the remaining letters were published as a second book in late May, and the two books subsequently were consolidated into one.[12] The excellent expositions contained in the book merit reading today.

Each letter writer explained and defended a provision of the proposed constitution and ended with the name *Publius*. Hamilton in the Federalist No. 17 argued "it will always be far more easy for state governments to encroach upon the national authorities than for the national government to encroach upon the State authorities. The proof of this proposition turns upon the greater degree of influence which the state governments, if they administer their affairs with uprightness and prudence, will generally possess over the people."[13]

Opponents were fearful the supremacy of the laws clause would permit Congress to convert the proposed federal system into a unitary one. Hamilton, in the Federalist No. 33, sought to allay this fear: "If a number of political societies enter into a larger political society, the laws which the latter must enact, pursuant to the powers entrusted to it by its constitution, must necessarily be supreme over those societies and individuals of whom they are composed. It would otherwise be a mere treaty, dependent on the good faith of the parties, and not a government, which is only another word for political power and supremacy."[14]

Madison, in the Federalist No. 39, explained the fundamental law would establish a governance system that would be "neither wholly national nor wholly federal."[15] The reader should recall the words *confederation* and *federation* in the eighteenth century were used interchangeably. The Constitution's supporters termed themselves federalists in an attempt to appeal to persons opposing a strong national government.

The necessary and proper clause also was justified in the Federalist No. 44 by Madison, who supported the clause by explaining employment of the first alternative—assignment of specific powers to each plane of government—would have produced "a complex digest of laws on every subject to which the Constitution relates"; and the second alternative would involve enumeration of "the particular powers of means not necessary or proper for carrying the general powers into execution," and the "task would have been no less chimerical . . ."[16]

Madison in the Federalist No. 45 assured citizens fearful of the creation of a national leviathan by stressing "the powers delegated by the proposed constitution to the federal government are few and defined," and added in the Federalist No. 46 that "a local spirit will infallibly prevail much more in the members of Congress than a national spirit will prevail in the legislatures of the particular states."[17]

The Federalist Papers generally were influential in swaying public opinion and particularly influenced the views of delegates to the New York convention, as a number of members lacked a complete understanding of the reasons why each provision was included in the proposed fundamental law. Sixteen letters, signed *Brutus*, were published in the *New York Journal* between October 1787 and April 1788 to rebut the proponents' arguments. Available evidence suggests the letters were written by Robert Yates, a delegate to the Philadelphia constitutional convention and an associate of Governor George Clinton of New York. These papers were not published in book form as *The Antifederalist Papers and the Constitutional Convention Debates* until 1986.[18]

Brutus, in an October 18, 1787, letter attacked the necessary and proper clause and the supremacy of the laws clause, and concluded:

> It is true the government is limited to certain objects, or to speak more properly, some small degree of power is still left to the States, but a little attention to the powers vested in

the general government, will convince every candid man, that if it is capable of being executed, all that is reserved for the individual States must very soon be annihilated, except so far as they are barely necessary to the organization of the government. The powers of the general legislature extend to every case that is of the least importance—there is nothing valuable to human nature, nothing dear to free men, but what is within its power. It has authority to make laws which will affect the lives, the liberty, and property of every man in the United States; nor can the constitution or laws of any State, in any way prevent or impede the full and complete execution of every power given.[19]

The influential *Federalist Papers* did not allay the fear of many citizens the proposed fundamental law would create a strong national government. Thomas Jefferson wrote a letter to Madison, and implied the Virginia convention would not ratify the proposed document until a bill of rights was incorporated.[20] Proponents sought to convince the conventions in the larger states to ratify the document by promising the first action taken by Congress under the constitution would be the proposal of a bill of rights. The conventions in Massachusetts, New York, and Virginia ratified the proposed constitution with the proviso that a bill of rights be added as soon as the constitution became effective.

The Constitution was ratified when the New Hampshire ratification convention, the ninth one, approved the fundamental document in June 1788, and also recommended the addition of a bill of rights. Elections were held for presidential and vice presidential electors and members of the U.S. House of Representatives in 1788, each state legislature appointed two U.S. senators, and the new national government became effective in 1789. A bill of rights containing twelve amendments was proposed by Congress, and ten amendments were ratified by the states and became effective on December 15, 1791.

THE FUNDAMENTAL LAW

Elements of the unitary and confederate systems of governance are incorporated in the U.S. Constitution to form simultaneously a compound republic and a unitary government by granting Congress complete control over the District of Columbia and U.S. territories. The fundamental document delegates to Congress specific regulatory powers, including exclusive and concurrent ones, and one service provision power, the postal service. The 1791 ratification of the Tenth Amendment reserves all other powers not delegated or prohibited to the states and the people.

DELEGATED POWERS

Section 8 of Article I delegates the following powers to Congress:

> To lay and collect taxes, duties, imposts and excises, to pay the debts and to provide for the common defense and general welfare of the United States, but all duties, imposts, and excises shall be uniform throughout the United States;

> To borrow money on the credit of the United States;

> To regulate commerce with foreign nations, and among the several States, and with the Indian Tribes;

> To establish an uniform rule of naturalization, and uniform laws on the subject of bankruptcies throughout the United States;

> To coin money, regulate the value thereof, and of foreign coin, and fix the standard of weights and measures;

> To provide for the punishment of counterfeiting the securities and current coin of the United States;

> To establish post offices and post roads;

> To promote the progress of sciences and useful arts, by securing for limited times to authors and inventors the exclusive right to their respective writings and discoveries;

> To constitute tribunals inferior to the supreme court;

> To define and punish piracies and felonies committed on the high seas, and offenses against the law of nations;

> To declare war, grant letters of marque and reprisal, and make rules concerning captures on land and water;

To raise and support armies, but no appropriation of money to that use shall be for a longer term than two years;

To provide and maintain a navy;

To make rules for the government and regulation of the land and naval forces, suppress insurrections, and repel invasions;

To provide for organizing, arming, and disciplining the militia, and for governing such part of them as may be employed in the service of the United States, reserving to the States respectively, the appointment of the officers, and the authority of training the militia according to the discipline prescribed by Congress;

To exercise exclusive legislation in all cases whatsoever, over such district (not exceeding ten miles square) as may, by cession of particular States, and the acceptance of Congress, become the seat of government of the United States, and to exercise like authority over all places purchased by the consent of the legislature of the State in which the same shall be, for the erection of forts, magazines, arsenals, dock-yards, and other needful buildings;—and

To make all laws which shall be necessary and proper for carrying into execution the foregoing powers, and all other powers vested by this Constitution in the Government of the United States, or in any department or officer thereof.

Implied Powers. An argument erupted between individuals supporting a loose interpretation of the delegated powers and those favoring a strict interpretation. Hamilton, for example, maintained Congress was empowered to charter a national government bank, and Jefferson countered Congress lacked such a power since chartering a bank was not a delegated power. Congressional enactment of the Alien and Sedition Acts disturbed Jefferson and Madison. The latter in particular expressed his strong opposition to the acts: "The sedition act presents a scene which was never expected by the early friends of the Constitution. It was then admitted that the State sovereignties were only diminished by powers specifically enumerated, or necessary to carry the specified powers into effect. Now, Federal authority is deduced from implication;

and from the existence of State law, it is inferred that Congress possesses a similar power of legislation; whence Congress will be endowed with a power of legislation in all cases whatsoever; and the States will be stripped of every right reserved, by the concurrent claims of a paramount legislature."[21]

Implied powers are essential for implementation of expressly delegated powers. The necessary and proper clause, also known as the elastic clause, is the basis of the doctrine of implied powers enunciated by the U.S. Supreme Court in *McCullough v. Maryland* in 1819: "Let the end be legitimate, let it be within the scope of the Constitution, and all means which are appropriate which are plainly adapted to the end, which are not prohibited, but consistent with the letter and spirit of the Constitution, are constitutional."[22]

RESULTANT POWERS

Congress can utilize two or more expressly delegated powers to infer it possesses a resultant power. The national legislature, for example, expressly is authorized "to establish a uniform rule of naturalization," but it is not specifically delegated the power to regulate immigration. Congress also is granted constitutional authority to regulate commerce with foreign nations. This power, the power to regulate the naturalization of aliens, and the power of the Senate to confirm treaties with foreign nations negotiated by the president serve as the constitutional basis for regulation of immigration.

A second example is congressional use of its delegated powers to borrow funds and to coin money as constitutional authority to issue paper money.

THE SUPREMACY OF THE LAW CLAUSE

The reader should note that this clause, in common with the necessary and proper clause, does not delegate a power to Congress. A compound republic with a national legislature and state legislatures with each possessing concurrent powers is faced with the problem of conflicts of laws. To solve the problem, Article VI of the Constitution stipulates: "This Constitution, and the Laws of the United States which shall be made in Pursuance thereof; and all treaties made, or which shall be made, under the authority of the United States, shall be the supreme law of the land, and the judges in every State shall be bound thereby, anything in the Constitution or Laws of Any State to the contrary notwithstanding."

The lower U.S. courts and the U.S. Supreme Court do not always invalidate a state constitutional provision or statute facially conflicting with an act of Congress by opining the conflict is not the type conferring jurisdiction upon these courts. Furthermore, courts often negate only one or two sections of a state statute conflicting with a congressional statute and the remainder of the state statute remains in effect, unless it contains a provision for invalidation of the entire law in the event a section is found to be unconstitutional.

A significant number of congressional statutes do not contain an expressed preemption provision removing regulatory powers from subnational governments. In consequence, state courts and U.S. courts are called upon to rule whether these statutes are preemptive and whether each statute supersedes all state authority in the regulatory field or only part of it. Congress possesses the authority to reverse U.S. Supreme Court preemption decisions, but the number reversed by Congress is small.[23]

Justice Hugo Black of the U.S. Supreme Court in 1941 commented on the Court's difficult role in interpreting congressional statutes.

> There is not—and from the very nature of the problem there cannot be—any rigid formula or rule which can be used as a universal pattern to determine the meaning and purpose of every act of Congress. This Court, in considering the validity of state laws in the light of treaties or federal laws touching the same subject, has made use of the follow expressions: conflicting, contrary to; occupying the field; repugnance; difference; irreconcilability; inconsistency; violation; curtailment; and interference. But none of these expressions provides an infallible constitutional test or an exclusive constitutional yardstick. In the final analysis, there can be no one crystal clear distinctly marked formula. Our primary function is to determine whether, under the circumstances of this particular case, Pennsylvania's law stands as an obstacle to the accomplishment and execution of the full purposes and objectives of Congress.[24]

THE GENERAL WELFARE CLAUSE

This clause is misinterpreted by a number of observers as authorizing congressional enactment of any law promoting the general welfare of the United States. This clause does not delegate a power to Congress. The misinterpretation, if accurate, would mean the governance system of the United States is a unitary one in view of the supremacy of the laws clause that provides for the supersession of any provision in a state constitution or a state statute in direct conflict with a congressional act.

Congress is authorized by the Constitution to provide only one service, the postal service, on other than federal property within states; state and local governments provide all other services. It is important to note the Constitution does not delegate authority to Congress to exercise the common law police power, as it is the exclusive reserved power of states to regulate individuals and property in order to promote and protect public health, safety, welfare, morals, and convenience. However, Congress encourages provision of services by subnational governments and influences their nature by means of conditional grants-in-aid, and employs its interstate commerce regulatory power to protect public health, safety, welfare, and morals of citizens.

CONGRESSIONAL PREEMPTION

Delegated powers can be exercised by Congress at its discretion to enact statutes removing partially or completely and prospectively and/or retrospectively the regulatory powers of subnational governments in a given field.[25] The reader should note a preemption provision not based upon an expressly delegated power, such as one regulating migratory birds, can become effective by the president negotiating a treaty with a foreign nation and approval of the treaty by the Senate in accordance with Section 2 of Article II of the U.S. Constitution. Bills implementing free trade concordats with other nations in recent years have been termed *agreements*, such as the North American Free Trade Agreement, rather than *treaties*, as the former requires only an affirmative majority vote of each house for enactment, compared to a two-thirds affirmative vote in the Senate required for approval of a treaty.[26] Congress occasionally includes a savings clause in a statute preserving part of the regulatory authority of states in what otherwise would be a complete preemption act, or authorizes a state to regulate provided its regulations are equal to or stricter than the corresponding federal ones (minimum standards preemption).[27] In 2015, there were twenty-eight minimum standards preemption acts.

Critics object to the costs imposed upon states and local governments by preemption statutes containing mandates requiring subnational governments to initiate specified actions, and restraints prohibiting these units to initiate specified actions. Some critics are convinced subnational governments are becoming little more than administrative subdivisions of the national government. Many complaints about federal mandates and federal restraints in fact do not involve preemption and are the result of subnational governments applying for and accepting federal conditional financial grants-in-aid.

Politically powerful special interest groups are responsible for a number of important preemption statutes. The environmental movement in particular became strong in the 1960s, and helped to persuade President Lyndon B. Johnson to send a message to Congress in 1967, recommending enactment of an air-quality statute removing all air pollution regulatory powers from the states. Governor Nelson A. Rockefeller of New York led a campaign to forestall enactment of such a law, and proposed as an alternative a series of interstate compacts, including the Mid-Atlantic-States Air Pollution Control Compact that was enacted by the Connecticut, New Jersey, and New York state legislatures, but did not receive congressional consent. Congress decided not to enact a complete preemption act, and instead enacted the Air Quality Act of 1967 allowing states to continue to regulate air pollution abatement, except emissions from motor vehicles, provided state standards are at least as stringent as the national standards and are enforced by qualified personnel who possess the necessary equipment.[28]

The motor vehicle manufacturers in the mid-1960s were facing the spread of non harmonious state emissions standards, feared they might have to develop as many as fifty emission control systems, and lobbied Congress to enact the proposed Air Quality Act of 1967. California had stricter motor vehicle air-quality emission standards than the proposed national standards, and the California standards would have been superseded if the proposal law was enacted. California lobbied Congress for an exemption that was incorporated in the act.

Preemption statutes remove regulatory powers from states, yet the latter do not always oppose enactment of such statutes, and occasionally a number of governors request Congress to enact a specific preemption act. For example, the National Governors Association requested Congress to enact the Commercial Motor Vehicle Safety Act of 1986, because states could not solve the problem created by drivers of commercial vehicles holding operating licenses issued by more than one state and continuing to drive after state revocation of their license for dangerous driving by utilizing a license issued by a sister state.[29]

Preemption statutes most commonly are based upon the interstate commerce clause, but other preemption statutes are based upon constitutional authority granted to Congress to enact laws relating to bankruptcy, copyrights, foreign commerce, naturalization, patents, and taxation. A preemption statute's coverage may be broadened by enactment of amendments as illustrated by the Clean Air Act Amendments of 1990.[30] Each of a small number of preemption laws contains a sunset clause providing for the expiration of the law on a specified date unless Congress extends the expiration date.[31] A preemption statute may be short—less than one page—or several hundred pages in length.

A recent trend is congressional inclusion of a preemption statute in another larger statute that otherwise is not preemptive, such as an appropriation act and an omnibus budget reconciliation act that are hundreds of pages in length. Examples include the Commodities Futures Modernization Act of 2000 in the Consolidated Appropriations Act for Fiscal year 2001, Satellite Home Viewer Extension and Reauthorization Act of 2004 in the Consolidated Appropriation Act of 2005, and the Improved Security for Drivers' Licenses and Personal Identification Cards Act of 2005 in the Emergency Supplemental Appropriations Act for Defense, the Global War on Terror, and Tsunami Relief Act of 2005.

TYPES

Preemption statutes have created a complex body of laws. Such statutes may be classified by type as complete, partial, and contingent. The first type removes all state regulatory authority in a given regulatory field, but may allow states to cooperate in the enforcement of the act. An examination of such statutes reveals there are eighteen subtypes, including ones depended upon state assistance for the achievement of their respective goal(s).[32]

Partial preemption statutes are of four types: Such a statute may (1) occupy part of a specified regulatory field; (2) establish minimum regulatory standards allowing a state-granted regulatory primacy by the U.S. Environmental Protection Agency (EPA) or the U.S. Department of the Interior to continue to regulate the field completely, provided its standards meet or exceed the national ones and are enforced; (3) authorize a state to establish a more stringent regulatory standard in a particular field without advanced approval of a U.S. department or an agency; or (4) permit a state to establish a more stringent procedural standard in a specified field without advanced federal approval. Fifteen more stringent state regulatory standards preemption acts and one more stringent state procedural standards act have been enacted to date. The latter act is the first of its type, and is contained in the Hazardous Materials Transportation Safety and Security Reauthorization Act of 2005.[33]

The year 1965 was turning point in the nature of the federal system when Congress employed in the Water Quality Act a new type of partial preemption termed *minimum standards preemption*, a state-federal partnership approach, encouraging states to employ their latent reserved regulatory powers in specified areas provided each state's standards are at least as stringent as the federal ones, and the state has qualified employees and necessary equipment.[34]

To obtain primacy with respect to water pollution abatement, for example, a state must enter into a memorandum of agreement with the U.S. Environmental Protection Agency. States granted regulatory primacy by a U.S. department or an agency are exclusively responsible for regulating, and the concerned national agency's roles are monitoring state performance and providing financial and technical support. This type also may be viewed as congressional devolution of power to the states. A number of congressional statutes, such as the Oil Pollution Act, do not contain authorization for the administering federal department or agency to delegate regulatory primacy to states.

ENACTMENT PACE

Congress enacted its first two preemption statutes in 1790: the Copyright Act and the Patent Act.[35] The enactment pace subsequently was slow, with only 29 acts enacted by the end of the nineteenth century. Such statutes continued to be enacted at a slow pace during the first five decades of the twentieth century: 14 (1900–09), 22 (1910–19), 17 (1920–29), 31 (1930–39), 16 (1940–49), and 24 (1950–59). The enactment pace increased sharply, commencing in 1965: 47 (1960–69), 102 (1970–79), 93 (1980–89), 84 (1990–99), and 160 (2000–09). By January 1, 2015, 711 preemption statutes had been enacted since 1790.

The number of preemption acts enacted during any given time period is not an accurate indicator of the amount and importance of regulatory authority removed from states and their political subdivisions. President George W. Bush, for example, approved 133 preemption acts in the period 2001 to 2008, yet relatively little exercised regulatory powers were removed from states, although each of the three Internet tax freedom acts prevent states from levying and collecting Internet access taxes.[36]

Congress responded to state and local government officers' criticisms of unfunded mandates by enacting the Unfunded Mandates Reform Act of 1995, establishing mandatory procedures Congress must follow to enact mandates, but not forbidding the enactment of such mandates.[37]

Congress also enacted the Safe Drinking Water Act Amendments of 1996, offering relief from the expensive filtering mandates that were forcing small local governments either to file for bankruptcy protection or to abandon their drinking water supply systems, and also were imposing major financial burdens on larger local governments.[38]

ADMINISTRATIVE AGENCY PREEMPTION

Many preemption statutes authorize the secretary of a department or the administrator of an administrative agency to promulgate regulations preempting related state and local government laws and administrative rules and regulations. This so-called administrative preemption tends to be resented by state and local government officers, and is controversial. The U.S. Supreme Court in 1961 sanctioned a deferential standard of review of federal agency administrative regulations and agency preemption of a state or local government law.[39] Nina A. Mendelson, in 2008, presented a strong case for a much more limited deference, noted the "lack of statutory guidance to agencies" relative to their preemption powers, and concluded that "a presumption against agency presumption is likely to result in more explicit congressional decisions on when agency preemption decisions are appropriate and what criteria should guide them. Asking Congress for that guidance may not only result in a more thoughtful focus on state regulatory autonomy, but may also help improve the administrative process."[40]

State and local government officers' resentment of federal preemption is directed in particular at what is termed *preemption by preamble*, which refers to a federal department or agency basing its preemptive regulations on the preamble to a statute declaring its goals. Congress, in 2008, specifically forbade the Consumer Product Safety Commission to preempt state or local government laws and administrative regulations on the basis of the preamble to a preemption statute.[41]

SIGNIFIANCE OF PREEMPTION

The drafters of the U.S. Constitution designed Congress with the expectation that it would employ its latent delegated regulatory powers and become the supreme regulator adjusting the nature of the federal union to meet existing and emerging challenges and problems. Extensive congressional enactment of preemption statutes since 1965 has produced without constitutional amendments a major governance revolution transforming the nature of the national economic union and the national political union. Many important changes are attributable to post-1964 innovative preemption statutes examined in this volume. Noteworthy developments are congressional enactment since 1976 of preemption statutes economically deregulating the airline, bus, motor carrier, natural gas, railroad, and telecommunications industries. Other preemption statutes since 1978 regulate states as polities.

Preemption statutes, particularly environmental regulatory ones, often are outline or skeleton laws establishing broad policy goals and delegating broad authority to secretaries of departments and administrators of agencies to promulgate detailed implementing rules and regulations. The enhanced role of bureaucrats in determining public policy raises questions relative to the democratic legitimacy of the policy-making process, as citizens have limited opportunities to influence the rule-making process compared to interest groups.

The local government plane, with its relatively small geographical scale, provides citizens with the greatest opportunity to exert effective influence during the policy-making process. To the extent that congressional preemption, directly or indirectly through the states by means of minimum standards preemption statutes, limits the discretionary authority of general-purpose local governments, participatory democracy will suffer. This conclusion is reflected in public opinion polls consistently revealing citizens generally have the highest respect for their respective local government and the least respect for the national government.

Congress finances in part programs established by preemption statutes by including in them unreimbursed mandates that often are costly and must be implemented by subnational governments. Several statutes also include restraints forbidding these governments to initiate specified actions and necessitating the use of costly alternatives. The Ocean Dumping Ban Act of 1988, for example, prohibits dumping of sewage sludge in the ocean and thereby requires municipalities located near an ocean to utilize the expensive alternative of incinerating the sludge or placing it in a landfill.[42] The Unfunded Mandates Reform Act of 1995 has not provided relief to state and local government from such mandates and restraints.[43] On the other hand, the Safe Drinking Water Amendments of 1986 offer major relief to public suppliers of drinking water, particularly small suppliers.[44]

Regulatory decision-making has become more centralized in Congress, which has become a unitary government in fields it has completely preempted. States nevertheless retain a broad range of regulatory powers, and continue to enact innovative statutes that subsequently are enacted by Congress and sister states. The national government somewhat surprisingly directly administers few programs it did not administer prior to 1965, and continues to rely heavily upon states for assistance in emergencies, inspections, and enforcement of national regulatory standards, planning, and technical assistance.

States generally continue to regulate effectively in partially preempted fields and occasionally demonstrate the inadequacy of enforcement by a national department or agency, as illustrated by New York State Attorney General Eliot Spitzer, who employed a decades-old state law to sue successfully the ten largest Wall Street brokerage firms for fraud.[45] The U.S. Securities and Exchange Commission, charged with administering ten regulatory statutes, was embarrassed by Spitzer's success in this suit and other suits.

Available evidence indicates Congress will continue to enact preemption statutes, some with innovative state opt-in and/or opt-out provisions, at a relatively rapid pace to cope with problems flowing from growing globalization of the U.S. economy, free trade agreements with foreign nations, interest group lobbying, and technological developments. The foci of such statutes probably will be banking, consumer protection, communications, environmental protection, financial services, and protection from terrorists. If state legislatures fail to harmonize their statutes levying taxes upon interstate commerce, it is probable that Congress will more frequently break its silence on such taxation by enacting preemption statutes.[46]

This volume primarily focuses on congressional enactment of environmental minimum standards preemption acts designed to protect and improve the quality of water, air, drinking water, and surface mining by removing all regulatory powers from states in these fields and subsequently devolving regulatory primacy to states that adopt regulatory standards meeting or exceeding the federal standards and have the necessary qualified personnel and equipment. Congress also has enacted twenty-four other minimum standards acts that do not devolve regulatory primacy, but allow states to regulate provided their respective standards are the same as or stricter than the federal ones.

ADMINISTRATIVE REGULATORY STRUCTURE

The best administrative structure for a federal or a state regulatory body is a subject of controversy.[47] The body may be organized as a multimember independent commission or as a single-headed department or as a bureau within a department. Various arguments are advanced in favor of each of the alternatives. The U.S. General Accounting Office (GAO) reported in 1987 it found no objective criteria employable to determine the best administrative structure.[48]

Proponents of commissions maintain the appointment of commissioners for long terms facilitates their development of expertise, ensures organizational stability, and permits the representation of multiple interests. The GAO, however, found a lack of stability in chairpersons and executive directors of the U.S. Consumer Product Safety Commission, and a diversity of members' opinions on issues.[49]

The single-headed agency, according to its advocates, improves the decision-making process as the agency can act quicker than a commission, in part because an expert administrator understands complex technical issues.

Robert S. Adler in 1989 concluded the Consumer Products Safety Commission should be restructured, but it should not be made a part of a department, as the commission's visibility and independence would be reduced.[50] He suggested conversion of the commission into an agency such as the Environmental Protection Agency. His suggestion has not been adopted by Congress.

Another important administrative issue is the scope of each commission's or agency's powers. Individual agencies and commissions focusing on a single subject in theory should devote more attention to their respective assigned responsibilities. Should each commission or agency focus on a single area—product safety is an example—or on broader related concerns such as drugs, the environment, food, and product safety? Other observers, relying upon the concept of span of control, maintain too many departments, and agencies report directly to the president or the governor of a state; the span should be reduced by placing these regulatory agencies or commissions in departments.

Relative to environmental protection, the Secretary of the Interior is responsible for the administration of the Surface Mining and Reclamation Act; and the administrator of the Environmental Protection Agency is responsible for the administration of the Clean Air Act, the Clean Water Act, and the Safe Drinking Water Act. It should be noted, the Secretary of the Interior was in charge of administering the Water Quality Act of 1965 until the function was transferred to the newly created Environmental Protection Agency in 1970.

Douglas R. Williams in 2013 recommended "federal regulatory authority be allocated to relatively autonomous regional institutions . . . vested with regulatory authority equivalent to, but in important ways more extensive than, the authority currently exercised by EPA."[51] This proposal clearly has a degree of merit, as the nature of environmental problems varies considerably throughout the United States, and a regional body would focus on the extent and the nature of the problems within its jurisdiction.

EXPANSION OF NATIONAL POWERS

Thomas Jefferson in 1814 was concerned that one plane of government would encroach upon the other plane. He wrote, "I have always thought where the line of demarcation between the General and the State governments was doubtfully or indistinctly drawn, it would be prudent and praiseworthy in both parties, never to approach it but under the most urgent necessity."[52] As the anti-Federalists feared, the powers of the general government encroached upon the powers of the states as the result of statutory elaboration of the delegated powers, generally broad judicial interpretations of delegated powers, and ratification of constitutional amendments delegating additional powers to Congress and ratification of the Seventeenth Amendment providing for the popular election of U.S. senators.

Congress in enacting statutes based on its delegated powers relating to subnational governments acts in one of three capacities: inhibitor, facilitator, and initiator. Congressional removal of all regulatory powers from states in a functional field illustrates its inhibitor role. Congress also facilitates state government actions by enacting a variety of statutes to assist them.[53] Congress acts as an initiator when it launches a new regulatory policy that may or may not be preemptive in nature. The congressional initiator role employs the leadership-feedback approach, by leading with a new policy and amending it, if necessary, based upon the feedback received from state governments, local governments, other organizations, and citizens.

The expansion of the powers of Congress concerned numerous citizens and convinced President Dwight D. Eisenhower to appoint the Commission on Intergovernmental Relations charged with conducting a major study of the distribution of power in the federal system. The commission focused on congressional preemption powers and concluded the conditions below justify the exercise of preemption powers:

(a) When the National Government is the only agency that can summon the resources needed for an activity. For this reason, the Constitution entrusts defense to the National Government. Similarly, primary responsibility for governmental action in maintaining economic stability is given to the

National Government because it alone can command the resources for the task.

(b) When the activity cannot be handled within the geographic and jurisdictional limits of smaller units, including those that could be created by compact. Regulation of radio and television is an extreme example.

(c) When the activity requires a nationwide uniformity of policy that can not be achieved by interstate action. Sometimes there must be an undeviating standards and hence an exclusively national policy, as in immigration and naturalization, the currency, and foreign relations.

(d) When a State through action or inaction does injury to the people of other states. One of the main purposes of the commerce clause was to eliminate State practices that hindered the flow of goods across State lines. On this ground also, national action is justified to prevent unrestrained exploitation of an essential natural resources.

(e) When states fail to respect or protect basic political and civil rights that apply throughout the United States.[54]

These criteria are basically as a restatement of the powers delegated to Congress by Section 8 of Article 1 of the U.S. Constitution and Section 5 of the Fourteenth Amendment.

The Commission also developed principles to guide congressional regulation to ensure states retain essential reserved powers:

First, the fact the National Government has not legislated on a given matter in a field of concurrent power should not bar State action.

Second, national laws should be framed that they will not be construed to preempt any field against State action unless the intent is stated.

Third, exercise of national power on any subject should not bar state action on the same subject unless there is a positive inconsistency.

Fourth, when a national minimum standard is imposed in a field where uniformity is not imperative, the right of States to set more rigorous standards should be carefully preserved.

Fifth, statutes should provide flexible scope for administrative cession of jurisdiction where the objectives of the laws at the two levels are substantially in accord. State legislation need not be identical with the national legislation.[55]

The first principle recognizes the constitutional law principle that Congress and state legislatures each may exercise concurrent powers. The second principle may be difficult to implement, and one may question whether the principle is functional in all situations. The third principle is a restatement of the supremacy of the law clause of the U.S. Constitution. The fourth principle is an important one that underlies congressional minimum standards preemption acts that date to the Water Quality Act of 1965 (now Clean Water Act, see chapter 2).[56] The fifth principle first was implemented in the Atomic Energy Act of 1959 that authorized the Nuclear Regulatory Commission to devolve certain regulatory powers to states signing an administrative agreement with the commission, provided the state statutes and administrative regulations are consistent with the federal statutes and administrative rules and regulations.[57] The commission did not criticize U.S. courts for their preemption decisions, but urged Congress to be more careful when enacting statutes not to preempt state regulatory powers unnecessarily.

Congress in 1959 created the U.S. Advisory Commission on Intergovernmental Relations that issued a 1984 report recommending Congress should enact a preemption statute only to achieve one of the following goals:

(1) to protect basic political and civil rights guaranteed to all American citizens under the Constitution;

(2) to ensure national defense and proper conduct of foreign relations;

(3) to establish certain uniform and minimum standards in areas affecting the flow of interstate commerce;

(4) to prevent state and local actions which substantially and adversely affect another State or its citizens; or

(5) to assure essential fiscal and programmatic integrity in the use of federal grants and contracts into which state and local governments freely enter.[58]

The above principles differ only slightly from the conditions identified by the Advisory Commission on Intergovernmental Relations nearly two decades earlier. President Ronald Reagan in 1987 released significantly different "Fundamental Federalism Principles":

(a) Federalism is rooted in the knowledge that our political liberties are best secured by limiting the size and scope of the national government.

(b) The people of the States created the national government when they delegated to it those enumerated governmental powers relating to matters beyond the competence of the individual States. All other sovereign powers, save those expressly prohibited, are reserved to the States and the people.

(c) The constitutional relationship among sovereign governments, State and national, is formalized in and protected by the Tenth Amendment to the Constitution.

(d) The people of the States are free, subject only to the restrictions in the constitution itself or in constitutionally authorized Acts of Congress, to define the moral, political, and legal character of their lives.

(e) In most areas of governmental concern, the States uniquely possess the constitutional authority, the resources, and the competence to discern the sentiments of the people and to govern accordingly. In Thomas Jefferson's words, the States are "the most competent administrations for our domestic concerns and the surest bulwarks against anti-republican tendencies."

(f) The nature of our constitutional system encourages a healthy diversity in the public policies by the people of the several States according to their own conditions, needs, and desires. In the search for enlightened policy, individual States and communities are free to experiment with a variety of approaches to public issues.

(g) Acts of the national government—whether legislative, executive, or judicial in nature—that exceed the enumerated powers of that government under the Constitution violate the principle of federalism established by the framers.

(h) Policies of the national government should recognize the responsibility of—and should encourage opportunities for—individuals, families, neighborhoods, local governments, and private association to achieve their personal, social, and economic objectives through cooperative effort.

(i) In the absence of clear constitutional or statutory authority, the presumption to sovereignty should rest with the individual States. Uncertainties regarding the legitimate authority of the national government should be resolved against regulation at the national level.

The Reagan principles are states' rights ones, emphasizing the roles played by the various states as laboratories of democracy, and advising Congress to exercise restraint in exercising its delegated powers. Richard S. Williamson, President Reagan's first assistant for intergovernmental relations, noted in 1982, the president was seeking "to change the presumptions which had been directing Americans and led them in recent years to turn first to the federal government for answers. He is seeking a 'quiet revolution,' a new federalism which is a meaning full American partnership."[59] Most interestingly, a review of President Reagan's record reveals he signed more preemption bills into law than any other president to date.[60]

AN OVERVIEW

This volume focuses on congressional enactment of four environmental minimum standards preemption acts designed to protect and improve the quality of water, drinking water, air, and surface mining by removing all regulatory powers from states in these fields, and subsequently devolving regulatory primacy on states that adopt regulatory standards meeting or exceeding the federal standards and have the necessary qualified personnel and equipment. Congress has enacted twenty-four other minimum standards acts that do not devolve regulatory primacy, but allow states to regulate provided their respective standards for each field are the same or stricter than the corresponding federal standards. The reader should note Congress also enacted contingent preemption statutes applicable to a state only if a specified condition(s) exists within the state, maximum standards preemption acts (see chapter 5), and state-friendly preemption statutes (see chapter 6).

Chapter 2 is devoted to improving water quality. Congress first established national minimum water-quality standards preemption in 1965 to solve the water pollution problem. In a related action, Congress in 1974 adopted national minimum drinking water–quality standards, and in 1977 enacted the Surface Mining and Reclamation Act to restore mine land and to prevent runoff from mined land entering waterways.

Chapter 3 focuses on minimum air-quality standards established by Congress and the U.S. Environmental Protection Agency.

Chapter 4 is devoted to maximum state regulatory authority standards and other statutes returning regulatory authority to states.

Chapter 5 examines state-friendly preemption statutes.

Chapter 6 draws conclusions as to the effectiveness of the various types of innovative congressional preemption statutes, with emphasis on their success in achieving their respective goals.

Chapter 2

Minimum National Water-Quality and Drinking-Water Standards Preemption

Congress enacted its first innovative preemption statute, the Water Quality Act of 1965, authorizing the establishment of minimum national regulatory standards, and granting a federal government administrator authority to delegate regulatory primacy to each state meeting or exceeding the national standards that has qualified personnel and the necessary equipment.[1] This chapter focuses on the Water Quality Act as amended, the Safe Drinking Water Act as amended, and the Surface Mining Act as amended.

Twenty-eight minimum standards acts as of June 2015 have been enacted and they may be placed in two classes. Each act in the first class regulates an entire regulatory field, such as water pollution abatement, and authorizes the U.S. Environmental Protection Agency or the U.S. Department of the Interior to devolve regulatory primacy powers within its respective sphere of responsibility to a state, provided it has standards at least as stringent as the national standards, and has the necessary qualified personnel and equipment to enforce the standards. Each act in the second regulatory class establishes minimum national standards that states must meet if they wish to continue to regulate in the concerned field, but there is no authorization for a federal government administrator to devolve regulatory primacy.

A brief survey of congressional conditional financial assistance to states will facilitate an understanding of the reasons why Congress in 1965 decided minimum national standards preemption was necessary to abate water pollution in place of the then-current command and control system.

FEDERAL FINANCIAL ASSISTANCE TO STATES

Congress first provided fiscal assistance to the states in 1790, by assuming the debts incurred by each state in fighting the war of independence.[2] An 1803 act admitted the Ohio Territory to the Union as a state, authorized a grant of federal land to the new state, and stipulated one section of land in each local political subdivision must be used for school purposes.[3] Congress in the same year decided to appropriate annually $200,000 to the states to assist in the arming and equipping their respective militia.[4] The U.S. Treasury accrued a large surplus from import duties by 1837, and Congress in that year decided to distribute the surplus to states as unconditional grants-in-aid.[5]

Congress in 1818 admitted the Territory of Illinois to the Union, and directed that 5 percent of the net proceeds of federal lands sold in the state must be transferred to the state for the construction of roads and "encouragement of learning."[6] The 1862 Morrill Act was the largest congressional land grant, and stipulated the U.S. government land be sold to raise funds for the establishment of state colleges of agriculture and mechanical arts.[7]

The origin of continuing national grants-in-aid with attached conditions designed to influence state government actions dates to the Hatch Act of 1887, which authorized grants to establish agricultural experiment stations at state colleges of agriculture.[8] The Carey Act of 1894 is the first act to contain a condition other than a purpose—preparation of a comprehensive plan for irrigation of arid land.[9] Grants-in-aid, with a few exceptions, require the recipient state or local government to provide matching funds, most commonly on a two-thirds national and one-third state government or local government basis. This requirement dates to the Weeks Act of 1911 that authorized grants for state forestry programs.[10] A second condition authorizes national government officers to inspect state programs financed in part with federal funds.

The Federal Road Aid Act of 1916 established the "single state agency" requiring each grant-in-aid must be administered by one state agency.[11] The act was amended in 1921, to authorize the Secretary of Agriculture to evaluate the competence of state highway department staff receiving federal grants.[12]

The increasing number of federal grants for highway construction raised the question of whether recipient states were diverting revenue produced by state highway user taxes to other purposes. To present a diversion, the Hayden-Cartwright Act of 1934 added a maintenance-of-effort condition penalizing a state for such diversions by withholding one-third of the federal highway aid a diverting state is eligible to receive.[13]

State and local government personnel historically were hired on a political patronage basis rather than on the basis of their respective competence. Congress became concerned that competent and politically neutral state and local government employees did not always administer programs financed in part with national funds. In consequence, the Social Security Act of 1935 required subnational government employees administering programs with funds provided by the act must be selected and promoted on the basis of merit.[14] Congress in 1939 and 1940 enacted statutes prohibiting state and local government employees to engage in partisan political activities if national funds finance any part of their salaries.[15] Congress gradually expanded the number of conditional grant-aid-programs until the early 1960s, when there was a sharp increase in the number of grants influencing more significantly state policy-making.

This chapter focuses in particular on congressional statutes authorizing a U.S. government department or an agency to promulgate minimum regulatory standards that may be exceeded by state laws and/or administrative regulations and rules. However, the reader should note that courts may interpret a congressional grant of regulatory authority to a U.S. department or an agency to be authority to promulgate only minimum standards. For example, the Federal Food, Drug, and Cosmetic Act of 1938 contains no reference to minimum national standards.[16] Nevertheless, the U.S. District Court for the Southern District of Illinois opined in 2001 that "FDA's labeling decisions impose only 'minimum' standards that are open to supplementation by state law through a jury's verdict enforcing a manufacturer's common law duty to warn."[17]

GENERAL WATER QUALITY

Congress in the 1870s became concerned by the outbreak of water-borne diseases and in 1879 established a national board of health authorized to collect and disseminate advice and information for a period of four years.[18] The next congressional environmental action was the River and Harbor Act of 1886, the first act to address water pollution by prohibiting the dumping of refuse in rivers; the act was recodified by the Rivers and Harbors Act of 1899.[19] Subsequently, Congress generally relied upon conditional grants-in-aid to assist states in abating water pollution for many years, but finally concluded reliance upon state and local governmental corrective actions encouraged by the "carrots" of such grants-in-aid would not solve the nation's serious water pollution problem. Encouraged by the growing environmental movement, Congress enacted the Water Quality Act of 1965 (now Clean Water Act).[20]

This act was the first of twenty-eight innovative preemption acts employing minimum national standards. The act requires each state desiring to continue to be responsible for water pollution abatement to adopt (1) "water quality standards applicable to interstate waters or portions thereof within such state" that meet or exceed the national minimum standards promulgated by the U.S. Water Pollution Control Administration, now the Environmental Protection Agency, and (2) to have an implementation and enforcement plan, qualified enforcement personnel, and the necessary equipment.[21] If a state fails to apply for regulatory primacy or fails to meet the act's conditions, the EPA becomes responsible for implementing the act in the state. The EPA's roles in a state-granted regulatory primacy are limited to monitoring state compliance with the national standards, and providing grants-in-aid and technical assistance upon state request.

Each state utilizes its EPA approved standards to assess water quality. These standards include designated uses, such as drinking or swimming, for each water body, threshold criteria protecting humans and fish from dangerous levels of pollution, and an antidegradation policy to prevent waters from deteriorating in terms of their respective quality. Waters are classified as good, threatened, or impaired. Sources of impairment include agricultural run-off, and discharges from manufacturing facilities, sewage treatment plants, and storm sewers.

Farm water runoff is a major source of pollutants, and illustrated by the approximately 300,000 dairy cows (6,000 cows per square mile) in the western sections of San Bernardino County and Riverside County in California.[22] There also have been major increases in the swine population in several states, including North Carolina, where the swine population increased from approximately 2.3 million in 1990 to approximately 10 million in 1998.[23]

States soon discovered it was difficult to develop statewide water-quality standards applicable to the various types of water bodies, such as small streams, major rivers, naturally muddy rivers, swamps, and other wetlands.[24] Weather conditions obviously affect water quality and may lead to violations of the minimum water-quality standards. These factors persuaded Congress to replace water-quality standards with a pollution discharge permit system in 1972 (see below).

Mark Atlas examined minimum standards preemption and explained:

The delegation to states of federal environmental programs can be viewed as a three-tiered principal-agent process. The first tier involves Congress, as the principal, delegating to the U.S. Environmental Protection Agency (EPA), as its agent, responsibility for developing and implementing an environmental program. The second tier involves EPA, now as the principal, delegating to its Regional Offices, as its agents, responsibility for implementing the environmental program in the states in their respective regions. The third tier involves EPA Regional Offices, now as the principals, overseeing authorized states, as their agents, as they implement the environmental program.[25]

Some observers view Congress's reliance upon state enforcement of federal environmental standards to be a weakness in view of the fact the EPA has limited resources to enforce the standards in the event a state fails to enforce them fully or returns regulatory primacy to the EPA.

This congressional minimum standards approach was revolutionary in 1965, and involves regulatory roles for both the national government and state governments.

Previously, a number of state legislatures were reluctant to impose more stringent water-quality standards for fear of driving polluting industrial firms from the state and making the state a less hospitable site for firms planning to construct new facilities or to relocate facilities. This approach meant there no longer would be states with low water-quality standards attractive to polluters.

A new type of national-state partnership is formed under this approach. Each state determines its standards with the proviso they must meet or exceed the national standards, and the role of the supervising federal agency, such as the EPA, is limited to monitoring state enforcement, and providing technical advice and grants.

Minimum standards preemption allows each state granted regulatory primacy to exercise discretionary authority tailoring its regulatory program to meet special conditions and needs in the state. Furthermore, the Water Pollution Control Act Amendments of 1972 directed the governor of each state to identify areas suffering water-quality control problems and to designate "a single representative organization, including elected officers from local governments or their designees, capable of developing effective area-wide waste treatment management plans for each area."[26] This act also established a permit system to regulate direct and indirect pollutant discharges, authorized citizen participation in the permitting process, and granted citizens standing to file suits to enforce the provisions of the act pertaining to violations of the effluent standards.

The coverage of the 1972 amendments was expanded by the Clean Water Act of 1977 that declared "it is the policy of Congress that the State manage the construction grant program under this Act and implement the permit programs under section 402 and 404 of this Act."[27] California in 1983 returned its primacy for the construction grant program to the EPA, "because state officials believed the EPA required more of primacy States than it did of its own regional officers who served as implementers in states that did not apply for or returned primacy."[28] Most states administer the national pollution discharge elimination system (NPDES), but EPA administers the system in Alaska, Idaho, Massachusetts, New Hampshire, New Mexico, U.S. territories, and certain tribal lands. The act also continued the grant of standing to citizens to file a lawsuit to enforce the act's provisions pertaining to violations of the effluent standards if the concerned state fails to enforce the standards.[29] Jennifer L. Seidenberg conducted a study of the NPDES system and concluded in 2006 that it "has been one of the most successful environmental programs ever undertaken in the United States . . ."[30]

The Water Quality Act of 1987 addresses "toxic hot spots" that are waters remaining toxic after the national water-quality standards have been met.[31] In addition, the act made storm water subject to the act's provisions. The Ocean Pollution Reduction Act of 1994, also referred to as the Clean Water Act Amendments of 1994, was enacted in response to the Exxon Valdez oil spill in Alaskan waters and added negligent discharges of oil to the list of criminal violations.[32]

By 2003, the EPA had delegated regulatory primacy to only Michigan and New Jersey for the Section 404 permit program relating to protection of wetlands, but had delegated regulatory primacy to forty states for the underground injection control program. The influence of the powerful farm lobby is revealed by the successful insertion of the following provisions in the 1977 act: "The Administrator shall not require a permit under this section for discharges composed entirely of return flows from irrigated agriculture, nor shall the Administrator directly or indirectly require any State to require such a permit."[33]

In 1993, Massachusetts launched a watershed initiative to improve identification of environmental problems and to improve the delivery of commonwealth agency services. This innovative approach encourages business firms, groups, individual citizens, and public officers to establish environmental protection priorities in their respective watersheds and an inventory of priorities utilizable by the secretary of the Executive

Office of Environmental Affairs to establish budgetary priories for the Commonwealth's environmental agencies.

Nonpoint source water pollution is the most difficult problem to control under the Clean Water Act because of runoff from agricultural lands and urban areas. In 1999, Scott D. Anderson argued in favor of an alternative approach to the act and recommended the Massachusetts watershed management and nonpoint pollution approach, as it "promises to improve upon watershed-based management programs of the past."[34]

A number of states complained there were significant differences between the EPA's regional offices in enforcing clean water standards. A 2009 U.S. Government Accountability Office report confirmed there were such variations, including inspections of facilities discharging pollutants, number and type of enforcement actions initiated, size of penalties accessed, and differences in the criteria utilized in determining penalties.[35]

THE STATUS OF WATER QUALITY

The EPA's Inspector General in 2003 published a report detailing the failure of the agency's water pollution abatement program by highlighting that the computer system is obsolete, contains inaccurate data, and omits thousands of the more than 64,000 sources of water pollution.[36] Nine days later, the EPA released another report revealing approximately 25 percent of the largest industrial plants and water treatment facilities violated the water-quality standards, and only a small number of plants and facilities had been fined.[37]

The EPA acknowledges it is difficult to determine whether water quality is improving, as individual states employ different methods to monitor and assess the quality of their respective water bodies, and their methods vary over time.[38] The EPA noted: "The science of monitoring and assessment itself changes. We know, for example, that a number of states have increased the amount of fish tissue sampling they conduct and as a result are finding more problems and issuing more protective fish consumption advisories."[39]

Robert W. Adler reviewed the experience of the Clean Water Act and concluded in 2010, it "has been among the nation's more successful environmental statutes. Where implementation tools have matched the statutory objectives, especially with respect to control of point source discharges of pollutants into surface waters, the law has resulted in significant progress in improving the quality of the nation's water."[40]

The GAO issued a series of reports since 2000 on the EPA's and states' enforcement of the Clean Water Act, and offered recommendations to improve enforcement. A 2009 report reviews the findings of the earlier reports, and concluded the EPA's regional offices were initiating inconsistent actions to enforce the act, including:

- inspection coverage by EPA and state enforcement staff varied for facilities discharging pollutants within each region;

- the number and type of enforcement actions taken by EPA's regions also varied, the size of the penalties assessed, and the criteria used in determining penalties assessed varied by region; and

- the regions' overall strategies in overseeing that the states within their jurisdiction varied, which may have resulted in more in-depth reviews in some regional programs than in others.[41]

The factors contributing to the differences included enforcement staff philosophical approaches, nonharmonious state laws and enforcement authorities, varied available resources to state and EPA regional enforcement offices, and EPA policies granting states flexibility in enforcement of standards. The EPA's ability to determine in more detail variations is attributable to inadequate and incomplete enforcement data. The report highlights the fact enforcement resources have not kept pace with increased responsibilities.

The GAO made a number of findings regarding the EPA including:

- overstating the impact of its enforcement programs by reporting penalties assessed against violators rather than actual penalties received by the U.S. Treasury.

- reducing the precision of trend analyses by reporting nominal rather than inflation-adjusted penalties, thereby understating past accomplishments.

- understating the influence of its enforcement programs by excluding the portion of penalties awarded to states in federal cases.

- annual amounts of injunctive relief and pollution reduction have not yet been achieved. They are based on estimates of relief and reduction to be realized when violators come into compliance.

• unclear legal standards . . . have hindered EPA's enforce-ment efforts.[42]

The report major's conclusions were funding for the EPA has not kept pace with its increasing responsibilities and action needs to be taken to strengthen its enforcement program.

Henry N. Butler and Jonathan P. Macey in 1996 drew upon experi-ence with cap and trade of emissions credits, illustrated by the regional greenhouse initiative (see chapter 3), and recommended congressional enactment of an amendment to the Clean Water Act authorizing issu-ance of tradable permits allowing "firms to benefit from being able to decrease pollution at reduced cost."[43] This approach involves establish-ment of a limit on emissions and authorization for firms emitting pol-lution lower than the limit to sell surplus emissions permits to other firms that need the permits to avoid exceeding the limit. This approach also encourages major polluters to replace aging pollution facilities and employ new methods to reduce emissions.

The GAO in 2013 issued a report on the Great Lakes Restoration Initiative (GLRI) to improve the health of the Great Lakes ecosystem that constitutes approximately 84 percent of the surface freshwater in North America.[44] An interagency task force of eleven U.S. government agencies was established in 2010 to devise a comprehensive approach to restoration of the health of each of the Great Lakes, and was supported by a congressional appropriation of approximately $1.3 billion.

In 2013, the GAO reported there was consensus among the GLRI participants that progress has been made in achieving GLRI goals, as illustrated by the removal of "the Presque Isle Bay area of concern from the list of areas of concern identified by the United States and Canada."[45] The report noted:

> . . . inadequate infrastructure for wastewater and storm water and the effects of climate change may lead to conditions that can negatively affect GLRI restoration efforts. One way to reduce the potential impacts of climate change is to invest in planning to reduce losses, rather than waiting for an event to occur and paying for recovery afterwards. The Action Plan touches on these factors, but it does not directly address how these factors may affect GLRI efforts to restore the health of the Great Lakes ecosystem or provide strategies to address them without more clearly expressing that connection in the next Action Plan, EPA will not be

able to help address the effects of these factors, including climate change, on GLRI efforts.[46]

SURFACE MINING AND RECLAMATION ACT

Environmentalists were disturbed greatly by numerous surface mining operations desecrating areas, destroying wildlife habitats, polluting waters, and causing flooding. The damage to the environment has been increasing because there has been a sharp increase in surface coal mining and a decline in underground mining in recent decades, with the former accounting for approximately two-thirds of the coal produced in the United States. The change in mining was not unexpected, as surface mining is less expensive than underground mining because the former facilitates the use of larger mining equipment and requires a smaller number of employees, thereby lowering costs. Among the mining states, Montana has coal reserves totaling 119 billion tons, and the largest producer, Wyoming, annually extracts 400 million tons of coal.[47]

The first state law regulating surface mining was enacted by the West Virginia States Legislature in 1939, and was followed by enactment of similar laws by Ohio in 1947, and by Kentucky in 1954.[48] It is apparent that the surface coal mining industry exerted sufficient political power to delay or reduce the severity of state regulation of such mining. Senator Everett Dirksen of Illinois in 1940 introduced a bill in the U.S. Senate mandating mining companies to restore mined land to premining contour, but no action was taken on the bill. Mining companies were opposed to congressional regulation and were joined by mining states. The companies admitted surface mining in the past caused environmental damage, but maintained current state regulations were adequate to prevent additional damage. Nevertheless, support for federal regulation increased in Congress, and it enacted in 1974 and in 1975 a bill regulating surface mining. President Gerald R. Ford vetoed each bill on the ground each bill would increase mining costs and add to inflation.[49]

Congress enacted and President James E. Carter signed the Surface Mining Control and Reclamation Act of 1977 (SMCRA), which regulates all aspects of surface coal mining, including site preparation and construction, mining operations, and final reclamation of the mined land.[50] The act was not the strong one environmentalists wanted, but it grants citizens authority to file a civil action in a court to compel a mining company to comply with the act, and levies a fee on every ton of mined coal to raise revenues dedicated to the abandoned mine reclamation fund that provides grants-in-aid to states to remedy problems attributable to abandoned mines. The reader should note the Clean Water Act authorizes EPA to regulate discharges of pollutants into interstate waters, and the discharge of dredged or fill materials into waterways requires a permit issued by the U.S. Army Corps of Engineers. Implementation of SMCRA led to many conflicts between mining companies and environmentalists. Several constitutional challenges to the constitutionality of the act were filed in courts, but none was successful.

Each state with coal-mined land may submit to the U.S. Secretary of the Interior a reclamation plan and an annual list of projects to be executed. The Office of Surface Mining (OSM) of the U.S. Department of the Interior administers the act and grants regulatory primacy to a state provided its regulatory program is consistent with the SMCRA. A state with an approved program receives a national grant of up to 80 percent of the first year cost of its reclamation program, 60 percent of the second year cost, and 50 percent for each succeeding year. Currently, only Tennessee and Washington of the twenty-six coal-mining states have federally administered regulatory programs.

Under primacy, only the state regulates surface mining as determined by the U.S. Court of Appeals for the Fourth Circuit in *Bragg v. West Virginia Coal Association* in 2001.[51] The OSM is responsible for monitoring the state's performance and providing technical assistance to the state. Should a state fail to implement its approved program, the state loses regulatory primacy and the OSM becomes responsible for regulating mining in the state. Title IV of the act authorizes a state granted regulatory primacy to administer an abandoned mine program. Citizens are granted standing by the act to file a suit against a state government granted regulatory primacy by the OSM.

No individual or firm, with two exceptions, may initiate surface mining operations without obtaining a permit either from the state agency granted regulatory primacy or the OSM. The owner of land may extract coal for his or her noncommercial use, and coal may be extracted as a part of a government financed construction project.

The Virginia Surface Mining and Reclamation Association challenged the constitutionality of the act as violating the Tenth Amendment to the U.S. Constitution. The challenge was rejected by the U.S. Supreme Court in 1981: "If a state does not wish to submit a proposed permanent program that complies with the Act and implementing regulations, the full regulatory burden will be borne by the federal government. Thus, there can be no suggestion that the Act commandeers the legislative process of the States by directly compelling them to enact and enforce a federal regulatory program."[52]

The act seeks to ensure mines are reclaimed and the environment is protected against problems such as water-quality degradation resulting from mining. The operator of a mine is required to post a performance bond sufficient to provide the state mining agency or OSM with adequate funds to reclaim the site should the operator fail to do so. The operator of a mountaintop coal mine also may have to obtain a permit under the Clean Water Act. The OSM possesses broad regulatory authority and delegated regulatory primacy to twenty-four states as of 2014, and also initiated a full national regulatory program in Tennessee after its state legislature repealed its regulatory program. Nine states with coal mine land decided not to seek regulatory primacy. OSM's field offices and regions develop, in collaboration with each mining state and tribe, a performance agreements/evaluation plans that must include, among other provisions,

- Program Evaluation goals and the plans to achieve those goals . . . ;

- State or tribal involvement in the oversight evaluation process;

- The National Measurement elements, including details of each review for:
  - Off-site impacts,
  - Reclamation success, and
  - Customer service;

- Other oversight activities that OSM may conduct in a state or on tribal lands . . . ;

- Inspection plans for the Evaluation Year, including the following information:
  - A description of what OSM expects to accomplish so that both the state or tribe and OSM staff understand the purpose of the inspection;
  - identification of the:
    — Number and type (joint, partial, complete, independent, etc.) of OSM oversight inspections, and
    — Method of selecting mines to be inspected (random or focused).[53]

OSM was assigned responsibility for establishing a bonding system and monitoring the system employed by each state to ensure mined land is restored properly.[54] The act specifies for each mine the area to be bonded, the amount and the type of bond, and the extent of the mining company's liability. The bond on a specified mining project is returned if the land is restored properly. This economic incentive approach to regulation has been successful, according to a 1988 study.[55]

In 2011, OSM published a document titled *Directives System* containing a wealth of information on the administration of the act.[56] The primary responsibilities of OSM when a state or a native American tribe has been granted regulatory primacy are to:

- monitor the state or tribe and conduct inspections of surface coal mining and reclamation operations to ensure that the state or tribe is effectively implementing, administering, maintaining, and enforcing its state or tribal program.

- ensure the state or tribe maintains its capability to fulfill SMCRA responsibilities.

- assist the state or tribe in implementing its responsibilities.

- report on the evaluation of the state or tribal program.

- work with states and tribes to resolve, in a reasonable and timely manner, program and implementation issues identified through oversight, and

- pursue corrective action provided by SMCRA, Federal rules, and OSM policy if states or tribes are not meeting program requirements.[57]

The office in exercising its oversight does not duplicate a state's or a tribe's program implementation responsibilities and focuses on the success of the program in achieving the stated goals of the act. Directive REG-23 stipulates the corrective actions for regulatory program problems and action plans.

THE CLEAN WATER ACT

The EPA is authorized by the act to regulate all pollutants discharged into navigable waters, including pollutants from surface mining. Furthermore, the U.S. Army Corps of Engineers has jurisdiction over dredged materials and fill discharged into waters. The EPA and the Corps work together to evaluate proposed discharges of fill material produced by surface mining.

The EPA issued a memorandum in 2011 pertaining to its review of Appalachian surface coal mining operations in EPA regions 3, 4, and 5.[58] The memorandum stresses it imposes no legally binding require‐ments, and is the result of environmental and health challenges that were unknown a decade ago, during which period 1,200 miles of streams were filled by surface mining activities. The memorandum also notes "deforestation has been linked to significant changes in aquatic commu‐nities as well as to modified storm runoff regimes, accelerated sediment and nutrient transport, reduced organic matter inputs, increased Algal Production, And Altered Stream Thermal Regimes."[59]

ASSESSMENT

Surprisingly, there has been relatively little recent research evaluating the effectiveness of the Surface Mining Control and Reclamation Act of 1977 in achieving its declared goals.

John C. Dernbach conducted a study of the impact of the surface mining program in Pennsylvania, and drew the following conclusions in 1986. He noted the act "is an ambitious statute," and listed his findings:

> First enforcement decisions in the new program are based on a comprehensive strategy that requires categorical enforcement responses to all violations . . .

> Second, Pennsylvania's new regulatory program is more open to outside scrutiny than the old program . . .

> Third, the State's Program is now managed and operated more professionally than it was under the old program . . .

> Fourth, the new program is primarily a written pro‐gram . . . Bureaucratic folklore and oral tradition do not provide as much clarity about program content as written requirements . . .

> Fifth, the new program establishes mechanical rules rather than judgment rules for many of its requirements . . .

> Sixth, the program provides for more and better information.[60]

He concluded, "there remains a lingering concern that the new program is sometimes unnecessarily systematized, inflexible, and oriented toward procedure."[61]

Charles E. Davis, Sandra K. Davis, and Denise Peacock published an article assessing the act in 1989 and noted: "Existing literature on state policy-making capabilities and OSM oversight of state agency performance is fragmentary, or out of date," and there are relatively few statistics on OSM oversight.[62] They reached a negative conclusion with respect to the OSM oversight:

> A more troublesome concern is raised by the assumption that federal oversight provides a useful check on state agency performance. Our analysis is admittedly short on data, but it does suggest that OSM's effectiveness in the 1980s has been compromised by high-level turnover, a lack of consistent policy direction, frequent reorganization and reassignment of personnel, the substitution of performance standards for design standards, a nonaggressive regulatory posture, and other management decisions that convey the impression that a commitment to SMCRA policy goals was lacking.[63]

Edward M. Green, a U.S. government attorney and a former counsel for the American Mining Congress, reported in 1997, he was "firmly convinced that SMCRA act has been, in the main, a successful example of the things that makes our country great—that is our unique ability to forge compromises that work."[64] He also noted court challenges of the constitutionality of the act failed.

The National Water-Quality Assessment Program released a report in 2000 on the impact of coal mining drainage in the Allegheny and Monongahela River Basins.[65] The report emphasized that 200 years of acid mine drainage (AMD) from coal mining have made 2,390 stream miles of the basin no longer capable of supporting fish communities.[66]

Robert W. Adler in 2003 published a long journal article—"The Two Lost Books in the Water Quality Trilogy: The Elusive Objectives of Physical and Biological Integrity"—highlighting the various sources of water pollution, and calling for the EPA "to revisit its virtually exclusive focus on chemical impairments to our aquatic ecosystems, and for Congress to revisit its policy of deference to the states in areas other than point source control of chemical pollutants."[67]

GAO in 2005 issued a major report on hard rock mining and coverage of reclamation costs.[68] The U.S. Bureau of Land Management (BLM) in 1990 "issued a policy instructing BLM officials to require operators to provide financial assurances for all plan-level operations and for notice-level operations if the operators had a record of noncompliance with federal regulations." Should an operator not complete the mandated reclamation, the BLM would initiate action to obtain the necessary funds from the financial assurance providers. The report revealed forty-eight hard rock operations had ceased, but were not reclaimed.[69] The BLM recommended that the Secretary of the Interior direct the BLM director to initiate two actions:

1. require the BLM state office directors to establish an action plan for ensuring that operators of hardrock operations have required financial assurances and that the financial assurances are based on sound reclamation plans and current cost estimates, so that they are adequate to pay all of the estimated costs of required reclamation if operators fail to complete the reclamation, and

2. modify LR2000 to ensure that it tracks critical information on hardrock operations and associated financial assurances so that BLM headquarters and state offices can effectively manage financial assurances nationwide to ensure regulatory requirements are met.[70]

In 2010, the GAO released the results of its study of surface mining in Kentucky, Tennessee, Virginia, and West Virginia. "Specifically, analyses have shown that (1) reforestation efforts at some reclaimed surface coal mine sites needed improvements; (2) surface coal mine sites have contaminated streams and harmed aquatic organisms; (3) valley fill may affect water flow; and (4) mine operators have not always returned mine sites to their approximate original contour when required to do so under SMCRA."[71]

The GAO issued a second report in 2010 on characteristics of mining in mountainous areas of Kentucky and West Virginia, noting citizens have limited access to information on surface mining activities and the future appearance of the reclaimed lands.[72]

In 2010, Will Reisinger, Trent A. Dougherty, and Nolan Moser reported Ohio, which had been granted regulatory primacy, failed to implement the act's bonding requirement, and this failure "highlights the inadequacy of backup federal enforcement."[73] They added other "parts of Ohio's surface mining program have been out of compliance since its inception in 1982, despite SMCRA's statutory requirement that OSM ensure that all state programs comply with the laws."[74]

Mining interests continue to express strong opposition to the act. President Mike Carey of the Ohio Coal Association in 2011 testified before the U.S. House of Representatives Subcommittee on Water Resources and Environment: "the Obama Administration and its allies have declared war on coal across all of Appalachia. We are ground zero for the fundamental overreach of the Obama regulatory agenda. They appear to be hell-bent on hurting those who work in the coal mining industry. The rural areas of Ohio, Kentucky, West Virginia, Tennessee, Illinois, Indiana, and Pennsylvania would be devastated from losing major employers such as coal companies."[75]

SAFE DRINKING WATER ACT

There are more than 53,000 public water systems in the United States that vary significantly in terms of the number of persons served, and a total of more than 300 million users. The operational costs of these facilities exceed $3.5 billion annually. Many local governments rely upon subterranean sources, as do a substantial number of homes with private wells. In addition, there are approximately 150,000 private drinking water systems. The average citizen in the United States daily uses in excess of 200 gallons of water, and the average residence consumers more than 200,000 gallons of water annually.

Many drinking water systems are old, and contain lead pipes representing a threat to public health, particularly to the health of children. Furthermore, water-borne diseases, such as cholera and typhoid, continue to plague the United States, where several million cases of acute gastrointestinal illness occur annually.[76] Long-term exposure to other contaminants—such as arsenic, chlorine, copper, lead, and nitrate are examples—also has harmful effects on citizens. The failure of the states to ensure quality drinking water increased pressure on Congress to act to solve the problem.

SAFE DRINKING WATER ACT OF 1974

Congress incorporated the minimum standards preemption and regulatory primacy approach in the Safe Drinking Water Act of 1974 (SDWA) that stipulates "a State has primacy enforcement responsibility for public water systems" provided the U.S. Environmental Protection Agency Administrator determines the state "has adopted drinking water regulations which . . . are no less stringent than" the national standards.[77]

The EPA administrator may grant regulatory primacy to a state if it has:

- regulations for contaminants regulated by the national primary drinking water regulations that are no less stringent than the regulations promulgated by EPA . . .

- adopted and be implementing procedures for the enforcement of state regulations.

- an inventory of public water systems in the State.

- a program to conduct sanitary surveys of the systems in the State.

- a laboratory that will serve as the State's principal lab that is certified by EPA.

- a program to ensure that new, or modified, systems will be capable of complying with State primary drinking water regulations.

- adequate enforcement authority to compel water systems to comply with NPDWRs . . .

- adequate recordkeeping and reporting requirements.

- adequate variance and exemption requirements as stringent as EPA's if the State chooses to allow variances or exemptions.

- an adequate plan to provide for safe drinking water in emergencies like a natural disaster.[78]

If a state fails to adopt or to enforce such standards, the EPA assumes complete responsibility for regulating drinking water in the defaulting state. Currently, all states except North Dakota, territories, and the Navajo Nation regulate drinking water.[79] The EPA regulated drinking water in North Dakota, and the other Indian tribes as of 2014. The agency's current policy focuses upon identification of water systems with serious compliance problems, and applies its enforcement resources to such systems. The 1974 act focused on treatment to ensure water was safe to drink.

A devolution provision in the act authorizes the EPA administrator, upon the application of a governor, to issue "one or more temporary permits each of which is applicable to a particular injection well and to underground injection of a particular fluid."[80]

The act exempts water systems servicing fewer than twenty-five persons or less than fifteen service connections that provide water to approximately one-half of the residents of rural areas. In other words, forty-five million persons receive water not subject to the act. Brigham Daniels, Erika Weinthal, and Blake Hudson are highly critical of the failure of Congress to extend the coverage of the act to these small systems.[81] They examined this problem by focusing upon arsenic in drinking water that is described as "an unaddressed threat to millions of small-users."[82]

The minimum standards regulation approach for underground injection wells also is employed by the act.[83] To obtain regulatory primacy, a state must declare illegal underground injections not authorized by a permit or a rule, ensure that authorized injections do not endanger drinking water, and conduct inspections of such injections.

SAFE DRINKING WATER AMENDMENTS OF 1986

Congress in 1986 amended the 1974 act by banning the use of lead pipes, solder, and flux in public water systems, and immediately became dependent upon subnational governments for the enforcement of the prohibitions.[84] Each state determines the best methods of enforcing the ban, but failure to enforce it may result in the loss of 5 percent of the federal safe drinking water grants-in-aid authorized by the amendments.

Congress in the same amendments extended the coverage of the act by establishing standards for subterranean water sources.[85] The EPA previously relied upon enforcement authority scattered in various sections of the *United States Code* and the *Code of Federal Regulations* to initiate corrective action to protect subterranean drinking water sources. The amendments direct the EPA administrator to establish maximum contaminant level goals and promulgate minimum drinking water-quality standards to expedite action to improve and protect the quality of drinking water.[86]

Included in the amendments were several expensive mandates whose implementation, particularly the filtration requirements, would impose major costs on large cities. The amendments also threatened to bankrupt many small local governments providing public water and to place a major financial burden on larger local governments. The act authorizes the EPA to enforce the standards promptly if a state has not commenced implementation action within thirty days of receipt of notification by the administrator the public water system must comply with the national minimum standards.

The potential impact of the amendments was clear with respect to New York City, which obtains drinking water from large reservoirs in the Catskill Mountains, located approximately 90 to 120 miles northwest of the city. To meet the national drinking water-quality mandates, the city was faced with the alternative of constructing a water filtration plant in the Bronx at an estimated cost of two billion dollars, or providing funds to small towns and villages in the reservoir drainage area to construct modern sewage treatment plants and working with farmers to eliminate drainage of fertilizer and manure into the reservoirs. The city chose the second alternative.

SAFE DRINKING WATER ACT AMENDMENTS OF 1996

These amendments emphasized protection of water sources, training of water plant operators, and provision of federal funds to assist in the financing of water system improvements. Congress also provided relief from the burdensome mandates by requiring limitations on new contaminants must be based on risk to human health, the cost of compliance must be considered, all drinking water must be assessed for susceptibility to contamination, and customers must be provided with information on the quality of drinking water.[87] The EPA regulates approximately eighty drinking water contaminants that might be found in public drinking water systems, and establishes a "maximum contaminant level goal" for each one.

In particular, the amendments addressed the water problems of small local governments, thereby removing the necessity for these governments to choose between filing for municipal bankruptcy protection or to close their public water systems. The amendments also removed a major financial burden from large cities, which no longer were required to filter their public water provided other actions, such as watershed protection, were initiated to ensure high water quality, including prevention of runoff from farms into water reservoirs.

The amendments stipulate that "in considering the appropriate level of regulation for contaminants in drinking water, risk assessment, based on sound and objective science, and benefit-cost analysis are important analytical tools for improving the efficiency and effectiveness of drinking water regulation to protect human health."[88] In addition, the EPA administrator is required to establish health standards for twenty-five additional contaminants during each three-year period, and specifically is directed to establish standards for arsenic, sulfate, and radon in drinking water.[89] State governments and local governments are authorized to establish priorities and to dedicate their resources to solving drinking water problems presenting the greatest threats to public health. For the first time, each supplier of drinking water must provide consumers with information on the source(s) of its water and its quality, and notify consumers promptly if there is a violation of the quality standards.

Small public water systems no longer are required to test for contaminants that never have been found provided they obtain a waiver from their respective state. The act allow states, which exercise primary enforcement responsibility for water quality, to grant a variance to each public water system serving 3,300 or fewer persons that cannot meet the "affordability criteria" established by the EPA Administrator, provided the terms of the variance adequately protect public health.[90]

The amendments address the New York City water supply system by authorizing financial assistance up to 50 percent of the cost of the protection program to enhance the quality of the water, and demonstration projects. In 1995, New York Governor George E. Pataki, New York City Mayor Rudolph Giuliani, EPA Region 2 Administrator Jeanne M. Fox, and local government officers in the Catskill and Hudson Valley regions signed an administrative agreement to protect the city's water supply, and thereby obviated the need for water filtration.[91]

By 1987, the EPA granted regulatory primacy to all states except Indiana and Wyoming. Iowa was granted primacy in 1977, but returned it to the EPA in 1981 because of the state's financial problems. When the problems were resolved in 1982, Iowa reaccepted primacy. Wyoming and thirty other states were delegated primacy for the underground injection control program under the Safe Drinking Water Act as amended.

Congress updated the Safe Drinking Water Act by a provision in the Public Health Security and Bioterrorism Preparedness and Response Act of 2002, mandating a community water system serving a population exceeding 3,300 to "conduct an assessment of the vulnerability of its system to a terrorist attack or other intentional acts intended to substantially disrupt the ability of the system to provide a safe and reliable supply of drinking water, and to prepare an emergency response plan."[92]

Robert M. Clark and J. A. Coyle in 1990 identified the following factors as affecting the quality of water in distribution systems: ". . . chemical and biological quality of source water; effectiveness and efficiency of treatment processes, adequacy of the treatment facility, storage facilities, and distribution system; age, type, design, and maintenance of the distribution network; and quality of treated water."[93] They also suggested the mixing of water from different sources and long-standing water in large systems may contribute to poor water quality.

The *New York Times* in 2009 analyzed federal data on drinking water quality and concluded more than 20 percent of the water treatment systems in every state violate provisions of the Safe Drinking Water Act as amended, yet most were not punished.[94] The bulk of the violations occurred in systems providing water to less than 20,000 residents. Drinking water since 2004 contains illegal concentrations of chemicals, including arsenic and/or uranium, and dangerous bacteria similar to bacteria in sewage. Research reveals these contaminants are responsible annually for millions of instances of illness.

The EPA issued its 2009 national public water systems compliance report revealing the incidence of state nonreporting of health-based violations was stable in the period 2006 to 2009.[95] Approximately 73 percent of the 111,196 water systems serving 81 percent of the population in 2009 had no significant violation of water-quality standards.[96] Systems in noncompliance decreased from 12,596 in 2006 to 6,626 in 2009. One-half of the reported violations involved the total coliform rule, which was the most common violation.[97]

The GAO released a report in 2011 revealing "data that states provided to EPA did not reliably reflect the frequency of community water systems violations of SDWA's health-based standards" in 2007 and 2008.[98] The office audited nineteen states and found they either did not report or inaccurately reported 20 percent of harmful violations the EPA determined should be reported. The GAO audited fourteen states in 2009 and found 778 health-based violations were not reported or were reported inaccurately. Funding restraints resulted in EPA in 2010 discontinuing its audits of violations data.

A second GAO report released in 2011 was highly critical of EPA's administration of the Safe Drinking Water Act as amended, and stressed that the "EPA has not effectively implemented the 1996 amendments requirement to consider, for regulatory determinations, contaminants that present the greatest public health concern."[99] The report was particularly critical of EPA's failure to prioritize contaminants based on the public health threat presented that reduces the agency's ability to reach regulatory determinations. The GAO observed: "In the absence of regulations or guidance for applying the broad statutory criteria, EPA appears to apply an informal policy that contaminants warranting regulation should occur in public water systems on a 'national' scale."[100] The EPA accepted GAO's recommendation pertaining to drinking water health advisories, but "did not agree to implement the remaining 15 recommendations we made, including an overarching recommendation that EPA develop policies or guidance that clearly articulate the agency's interpretation of the Safe Drinking Water Act's broad statutory criteria . . ."[101]

SUMMARY AND CONCLUSIONS

This chapter explains the origin of congressional minimum standards preemption of state regulatory authority in the Water Quality Act of 1965. These standards have been a major success in reducing point source pollution, according to many experts on water pollution abatement.

Minimum standards preemption has been most successful in forging a national-state regulatory partnership, allowing individual states to tailor the federal water standards law to meet the unique problems in each state and to adopt innovative approaches to solving the concerned problems. The Clean Water Act eliminated the previous "race to the bottom" under which individual states seeking to attract industrial firms lowered their water-quality standards, if any, for polluting firms, and had lax enforcement. The Surface Mining Act also reduced the amount of runoff from mining entering waterways. Unfortunately, acid mining drainage continues to be a problem and the act has had limited success in requiring the polluters to pay for the required restoration of the land. Furthermore, the innovative water-quality approach does not address the major water pollution problems flowing from the voluminous runoff of pollutants from municipal streets, farms, and lawns.

Nationwide, there have been significant improvements in the quality of drinking water since the enactment of the Safe Drinking Water Act of 1974. However, the evidence presented in this chapter reveals the need for additional improvements in drinking water quality.

Chapter 3 reviews the experience of minimum national standards preemption in abating air pollution.

Chapter 3

Mininum National Air-Quality Standards Preemption

Industrialization, increased consumption of electricity, and the large increase in the number of motor vehicles in the United States primarily were responsible for the serious air pollution problem in many sections of the nation during the first half of the twentieth century. Large city governments were the early leaders in air pollution control, when they commenced to regulate smoke emissions in the late nineteenth century; Chicago and Cincinnati enacted smoke control ordinances in 1881.[1] The Massachusetts General Court (legislature) created in 1910 the metropolitan smoke inspection district, covering six municipalities in the greater Boston area.[2] Air pollution control districts were established in the Los Angeles area in 1948 and such districts became more common elsewhere during the 1960s.

The increasing seriousness of the air pollution problem was highlighted by the so-called Donora disaster of October 26, 1948, when the townships of Donora and Webster in Pennsylvania were engulfed by a poisonous and thick cloud of smog resulting from a temperature inversion of industrial pollution. The U.S. Public Health Service subsequently conducted a study of the disaster, and concluded approximately 6,000 persons had "experienced some affection from the smog . . . Of these, 2,148 were mildly affected, 2,322 moderately affected, and 1,440 severely affected. In addition, there were 20 persons who died during or shortly after the episode."[3]

Charles O. Jones identified four factors impeding efforts to regulate the Donora polluters: (1) the Pennsylvania Department of Health lacked adequate statutory authority to initiate air pollution abatement programs; (2) state law defined "foul air" as a health hazard, an inadequate term; (3) lack of citizen groups lobbying for protection against air pollution; and (4) industrial leaders lobbying state legislators not to initiate actions that would inhibit production.[4] The Donora disaster was publicized widely, but did not lead to an immediate response by Congress.

The most major air pollution problems in the United States in the twenty-first century are caused by fine particles and ozone.

CONGRESSIONAL RESPONSE

Air pollution at the time of the Donora disaster generally was viewed as a state government problem and a local government problem. Nevertheless, Congress enacted the Air Control Act of 1955, authorizing the U.S. Public Health Service to conduct research on the problem, and to provide financial and technical assistance to subnational government air pollution control agencies.[5] The Clean Air Act of 1963 reasserted the primary responsibility of state governments and local governments to prevent and control air pollution, but the act also authorized the U.S. Public Health Service to engage in more extensive air pollution research, including interstate problems and national problems, and contained an enforcement provision.[6] The U.S. District Court was authorized by the act to order abatement of air pollution only after giving "due consideration to the practicability of complying with such standards as may be applicable and to the physical and economic feasibility of securing abatement of any pollution."[7]

MOTOR VEHICLE POLLUTION CONTROL ACT OF 1965

The act was prompted in part by state legislatures commencing to regulate emissions from motor vehicles in the early 1960s to reduce air pollution.[8] The motor vehicle industry immediately became concerned it might have to develop fifty specialized emission control systems to meet the different requirements of each state. The industry successfully lobbied Congress to remove from states their authority to establish emission standards for new vehicles.

The 1965 act completely preempted responsibility for the establishment of emission standards for motor vehicles, commencing with 1968 models. The secretary of Health, Education, and Welfare (now the Environmental Protection Agency administrator) was directed by the act to promulgate emission standards for moving sources in general and for motor vehicles in particular. The act required the secretary in developing standards to consider the economic cost and the technical feasibility of compliance with the standards.

The U.S. government does not need state and local government assistance to ensure emissions from new motor vehicles meet national air-quality standards. The U.S. government, however, is dependent upon state inspection of on-highway vehicles to determine whether they comply with the standards in states that have applied for and received regulatory primacy under the Clean Air Act's minimum national ambient air-quality standards (NAAQS).

AIR QUALITY ACT OF 1967

Congress, in this innovative act, adopted the minimum standards approach of the Water Quality Act of 1965.[9] A state is granted regulatory primacy provided its air-quality standards meet or exceed the federal minimum standards, and the state has the necessary qualified personnel and the necessary equipment. This act is the first comprehensive air-quality preemption act regulating emissions from stationary sources and mobile vehicles.

Included in the act is a provision, termed the California exception, added to the act because of the seriousness of air pollution in the state with strict regulatory standards to curb mobile sources emissions. Section 209b of the act directs the administrator of the U.S. Environmental Protection Agency to grant a waiver to California if its standards will be "in the aggregate, at least as protective of public health and welfare as applicable federal standards." Subsequently, other states were allowed to adopt the more stringent California standards.

The U.S. Government Accountability Office (GAO) in 2009 issued a report reviewing the EPA's waiver process for California and noted past decisions produced the following results:

- The majority of the waiver requests were granted in full—approximately 42 waiver decisions have been fully granted.

- Waivers were granted in part when EPA found that aspects of the waiver request did not meet the criteria under Section 209(b). EPA has granted waivers in part approximately nine times since 1967.

- Determinations that a waiver should be granted in part were usually based on the Section 209(b) criterion covering technical feasibility and lead time issues . . .

- Decision documents were drafted prior to announcements about waiver decisions . . . these documents are typically drafted after the public hearing and public comment processes are complete.

- Since the mid-1980s, Assistant Administrators generally signed the waiver decisions rather than the Administrators. Since 1992, it has been the official duty of the Assistant Administration for Air and Radiation to sign waiver decisions.[10]

The act, relative to other sources of air pollution, adopted the regulatory primacy approach of the Water Quality Act of 1965 by authorizing the Secretary of Health, Education, and Welfare (HEW) to delegate regulatory primacy to each state with the necessary qualified personnel and equipment, and state standards meeting or exceeding the national standards (see chapter 2). David M. Konisky and Neal D. Wood in 2009 commented: "Delegation thus enables states to strategically determine where to concentrate their enforcement efforts, providing an opportunity to perform less enforcement in areas bordering other jurisdictions."[11] Their research, however, did not discern any important differences in a state's enforcement policy in the area adjacent to another state(s), and were referring to international borders.[12]

The act also assigned the secretary the tasks of creating air-quality control regions in consultation with states and a joint federal-state procedure for developing ambient air-quality standards.

CLEAN AIR ACT AMENDMENTS OF 1970

These amendments represented a major change in the congressional policy relying upon the states to provide the necessary leadership and to consider the technical feasibility of various abatement control types by (1) superseding existing federal air pollution control statutes; (2) providing for direct federal government action to protect public health; (3) specifying explicit dates for state adoption of air-quality standards and abatement plans; and (4) initiating a dramatic new approach to solving the motor vehicle air pollution problem that did not consider the economic and the technical feasibility of achieving the mandated

90 percent reduction in emissions of carbon monoxide, hydrocarbons, and nitrogen oxides by 1975 model vehicles.[13]

The amendments declared: "Each State shall have the primary responsibility for assuring air quality within the entire geographical area comprising such State by submitting an implementation plan for such State specifying the manner in which national primary and secondary ambient air-quality standards will be achieved and maintained within each air-quality control region in such State."[14] The Council on Environmental Quality commented in 1973, the amendments "set in motion a nationwide Federal-State program to achieve acceptable air quality."[15] EPA approval of a state implementation plan allows the EPA to enforce the plan similar to the enforcement of a promulgated federal regulation. No changes can be made in the plan without EPA approval.

A key question must be answered by an environmental remedial statute. Should there be a transition period during which polluters may continue to emit pollutants while installing new pollution abatement equipment? Congress recognized installation of such equipment would be expensive and would be phased in over time, and decided to shield operating coal-fired electric power plants from regulation.[16] This exemption decision was subjected to strong criticism on the ground the exemption provided plant owners with an incentive to continue to use the old plants.[17] Modification of an existing facility would subject it to the act's strict emission standards. Older facilities also benefited from the authorization of the bubble concept, allowing old sources of air pollution to meet plantwide emissions standards.

The EPA administrator was directed to publish in the *Federal Register* within 90 days a list of categories of stationary sources of air pollution subject to the performance standards established under the amendments.[18] The administrator was granted an additional 120 days following publication of the list to include in the *Federal Register* proposed regulations establishing federal standards for new sources of air pollution. Each state was authorized to submit to the administrator a state implementation plan (SIP) containing the procedure for implementing and enforcing standards of performance for new sources of emission located in the state, and the administrator was empowered to delegate authority to each state to implement and enforce the standards for other than new U.S.-owned sources. On February 25, 1974, the administrator promulgated final regulations for reviewing the air-quality impact prior to construction of new facilities—labeled indirect sources—generating significant amounts of motor vehicle traffic. The regulations became effective on January 1, 1975.[19]

Sierra Club v. Ruckelshaus. The Sierra Club in 1972 successfully sued the EPA administrator in the U.S. District Court for the District of Columbia, seeking a preliminary injunction to enjoin him from approving any section(s) of a state air-quality implementation plan allowing significant deterioration of air quality.[20] The club's brief presented extensive arguments based on the language of the Clean Air Act requiring nondegradation and extensive congressional hearings on the proposed amendments expressing such a policy. The court's decision contained no definition of the term *significant deterioration of air quality.*

The EPA appealed the decision to the U.S. Court of Appeals for the District of Columbia Circuit, which upheld the lower court's decision, and the U.S. Supreme Court in 1973, by a four-to-four vote, denied a petition for the issuance of a writ of certiorari, and thereby let stand the District Court's decision interpreting the 1970 amendments as forbidding states to permit significant deterioration of air quality.[21]

The EPA was forced to implement a nondegradation program without statutory or judicial guidance. The agency initiated four actions, including the establishment of clean air zones and polluted air zones. Although pollution levels would not be allowed to exceed national standards in either zone, only minor increases in the degree of pollution would be allowed in the former zones, whereas larger increases would be allowed in the latter zones. Tom Tietenberg explained in 2010: "Prohibiting economic growth as the means of resolving air quality problems was politically unpopular among governors, mayors, and many members of Congress."[22] A better solution is the cap-and-trade approach described below.

Albert C. Hyde completed in 1980 a study of the development by the bureaucracy, including interagency group decision-making, of the nondegradation regulatory policy for pristine air zones.[23] Particular attention was placed by Hyde on interest group pressure on administrative agencies over a two-year period. The promulgated rules and regulations provide for the use of the primary and the secondary standards as one zone of allowable pollution, a second zone where a limited amount of deterioration is allowed, and a final zone where little or no deterioration is allowed.[24]

Environmentalists and industrialists were not satisfied with the promulgated regulations. Hyde noted: "The 1977 amendments incorporated much of the logic and concepts of the 1974 regulations," and "can be construed as vindication of the Agency's policy decision."[25]

CLEAN AIR ACT AMENDMENTS OF 1977

The amendments (1) provided statutory authority for the court's prevention of significant deterioration of air-quality decision, (2) focused primarily on prevention of significant deterioration of air quality in regions attaining the NAAQS, (3) established major permit review requirements to ensure attainment and maintenance of the standards, and (4) prohibited emissions from a state contributing to the nonattainment of the NAAQS in a sister state(s).[26]

In 1981, Idaho returned its air-quality regulatory primary authority to the EPA, but reaccepted the authority in 1983. Patricia M. Crotty commented, the EPA "assumed stringent enforcement within Idaho by contracting out supervisions to a private firm." These developments illustrate states will rescind their acceptance of regulatory primary "if it suits their respective political interests."[27]

Grahma Zorn in 2009 suggested Congress should consider replacing the prevention of significant deterioration program with an emissions trading program similar to the Clean Air Act's acid rain program (see below).[28]

CLEAN AIR ACT AMENDMENTS OF 1990

This 313-page act made important changes in the Clean Air Act. EPA was authorized, after consulting the concerned states, to establish interstate air-quality regions recognizing the existence of different types of air pollution problems in the various regions of the nation, and to assist the states in their efforts to reduce emissions. Each state must include in its strategies for reducing interstate pollution notification of sister states of existing or proposed sources affecting significantly air pollution beyond its borders. Similarly, the act has a so-called good neighbor provision requiring each plan to prevent any emissions contributing significantly to nonattainment in a neighboring state. The EPA in 2005 promulgated the Clean Air Interstate Rule (CAIR) to reduce the interstate effects of sulfur dioxide (SO_2) and nitrogen oxide (NO_x) emission from fossil fuel electricity generation plants.[29] The rule created a cap-and-trade program in states electing to participate. North Carolina challenged the rule, and the U.S. Court of Appeals for the District of Columbia Circuit in 2008 invalidated it.[30]

Five sections of the amendments specifically authorize governors to initiate corrective actions.[31] A governor convinced that the interstate transport of air pollutants constitutes a violation of a national ambient air-quality standard in his or her state may petition the EPA administrator to establish a transport region and a transport commission composed of EPA and state officers.[32] The administrator, at the requests of state governors, established the Ozone Transport Commission composed of representatives of twelve northeastern states and the

District of Columbia.[33] The Commission in 1995 developed the nitrogen oxide budget program, a cap-and-trade initiative designed to reduce NO_x emissions. Harry Moren conducted a study of the program, and in 2009 concluded it succeeded in reducing such emissions.[34]

Title II of the amendments relates to mobile sources of air pollution emissions, with many sections directing the EPA administrator to promulgate specific standards, enforceable by the agency, pertaining to subjects such as control of vehicle refueling emissions, misfueling, fuel volatility, and lead substitute additives. A most important amendment authorizes sister states to adopt California motor vehicle emission standards that are stricter than EPA standards.[35]

Title IV addresses the acid rain problems, attributable primarily to anthropogenic emissions of nitrous oxide and sulfur dioxide from coal-burning electric-generating plants. The mixture of the two oxides reacts to form nitric acid and sulfuric acid that are transported great distances in the atmosphere. Northeastern states and Canadian provinces in particular oppose the interjurisdictional transport of these pollutants. Midwestern and Appalachian states with high sulfur content coal oppose congressional enactment of acid rain statutes. The amendments establish a new control approach, cap and a trade, involving sharply reduced permissible emissions of NO_x and SO_2 (a cap), and authorization for a utility company whose plants release fewer sulfur dioxide emissions than the maximum allowed to sell sulfur dioxide credits on the open market to other utility companies needing the allowance to avoid exceeding their respective emissions limit.[36] EPA facilitated the implementation of the new approach by sponsoring an auction market conducted by the Chicago Board of Trade.

The market-based emission trading program, in contrast to the former command and control system, is a flexible innovative approach allowing every utility company to avoid fines by tailoring its compliance plans to the unique needs of each plant. The companies can employ the option of low sulfur coal, install new emission abatement equipment, and/or purchase allowances. The EPA in 2001 reported SO_2 had been reduced by more than 50 percent during the period 1995 through 1999.[37] The 2002 *Economic Report of the President* revealed the trading program "lowered emissions substantially while yielding considerable cost savings, especially compared with the previous command-and-control regime."[38]

A 2012 journal article reviewed the first twenty years of experience with the cap-and-trade approach, and concluded it is a major success that "seems especially well suited to address the problem of climate change . . ."[39]

REGIONAL GREENHOUSE INITIATIVE

The failure of Congress to regulate greenhouse gas persuaded Governor George E. Pataki of New York in 2001 to appoint a greenhouse gas task force to examine policy options. Its 2003 report recommended the establishment of an in-state cap-and-trade program.[40] Shortly thereafter, the governor wrote to the governors of the other northeastern states and suggested implementation of a regional cap-and-trade (RRGI) program to reduce carbon dioxide emissions. The governors established a working group that drafted an interstate memorandum of understanding (MOU), signed by ten Mid-Atlantic and northeastern states, establishing the Regional Greenhouse Gas Initiative (RGGI).[41] The MOU is an interstate administrative agreement, but is not one requiring the consent of Congress to become effective. The U.S. Supreme Court in *Virginia v. Tennessee* in 1893 opined the consent of Congress is required only for compacts tending to "increase the political power or influence" of member states and to encroach "upon the full and free exercise of federal authority."[42] The MOU does not authorize each signatory state to exercise a power the state could not exercise in the absence of the MOU or an administrative body to exercise the power, but the MOU does provide an individual signatory state may withdraw from the MOU.

The RGGI held its first carbon allowances auction in September 2008, but Delaware, New Jersey, New Hampshire, and New York did not participate. In December 2008, all member states participated in the auction.[43] A December 2010 auction produced $16.9 million in revenue for New York. In 2011, the California Air Resources Board placed a cap on the emission of greenhouse gas and established a system of tradable carbon allowances similar to the RGGI.[44]

ALTERNATIVE TO INTERSTATE SUITS

The Clean Water Act and the Clean Air Act each facilitates solutions to two types of interstate relations pollution problems. Prior to these acts, a downriver state or a downwind state suffering adverse consequences flowing from pollutants emitted in the upriver or upwind state had only one legal course of remedial action, and that was to file a petition and a supporting brief in the U.S. Supreme Court, seeking to invoke its original jurisdiction and its express permission for leave to file a complaint in equity against another state(s).[45] The Court uses its discretion to determine whether to invoke its original jurisdiction by inquiring whether (1) each party state is a genuine party or the complainant state is representing private parties, (2) the complaint is a justiciable controversy, and (3) the dispute is an appropriate one for the court to review.[46] The Court generally is reluctant to invoke its original jurisdiction as it interferes with what the Court considers to be its most important function, deciding appeals. The Court suggested in a number of instances the concerned states should seek to resolve their disputes by means of negotiations or an interstate compact.[47]

Justice Felix Frankfurter of the U.S. Supreme Court highlighted in 1939 the inadequacies of interstate litigation in terms of "its episodic character, its necessarily restricted scope of inquiry, its confined regard for consideration of policy, its dependence on the contingencies of a particular record, and other circumscribing factors."[48] Invocation of the Court's original jurisdiction is expensive for the concerned states and time-consuming as the Court appoints a special master to collect facts in the dispute and, if authorized by the court, to draft recommendations that could be incorporated in the court's degree.[49]

On a number of occasions, the Court opined Congress is better qualified than the Court to resolve interstate controversies. Relative to the Virginia prayer for the issuance of a writ of *mandamus* to enforce a previous judgment rendered in Virginia's favor, the Court in 1918 explained Congress has plenary authority to enforce the obligation of West Virginia, and decided to defer action on the prayer "in order that full opportunity may be afforded to Congress to exercise the power which it undoubtedly possesses."[50]

Under either of these two acts, a state suffering adverse environmental consequences of pollutants emanating from another state can pressure EPA to require the upstream or upwind state(s) to curtail the discharge of pollutants if they exceed the applicable national minimum standards.

EXPORT OF POLLUTANTS

Do states export air pollution by utilizing less stringent air pollution abatement enforcement in areas bordering another state? David M. Konisky and Neal D. Woods in 2009 published their answer to this question: ". . . we do not find evidence to support the contention that states enforce air pollution laws less stringently near state borders. However, we do find significantly weaker state air enforcement effort near international borders, providing evidence that states strategically allocate their enforcement effort in ways that serve to export pollution to Canada and Mexico."[51]

The Clean Air Act contains a good neighbor provision designed to reduce transmission of upwind state pollutants to a downwind state.[52] The EPA promulgated a rule in 2011, requiring each state to include in its SIP a provision designed to reduce transmission of fine particulate matter and ozone to sister states.[53] The rule was challenged, and the U.S. District Court for the DC Circuit vacated and remanded the rule because it violated the act by requiring the upwind states "to reduce emissions by more than their own significant contributions to a downwind State's nonattainment."[54] The U.S. Supreme Court in 2013 issued a writ of certiorari, and will examine and issue an opinion on the controversy.

COURT INTERPRETATION

State and U.S. courts have played important roles in interpreting the various congressional air-quality acts.

Nineteen private parties in 1999 petitioned the EPA to regulate greenhouse gases emitted by motor vehicles. Twelve states and other parties sued the EPA, which responded in 2003 by denying the petition and explaining it lack authority under the law to regulate greenhouse gases emitted by new motor vehicles.[55] An appeal was made to the U.S. Court of Appeals for the District of Columbia Circuit that in 2005 dismissed or denied the various petitions, and a writ of certiorari was issued by the U.S. Supreme Court.[56] In 2007, the Court, by a five-to-four vote, ruled Massachusetts had standing to bring the suit and the EPA possesses authority to regulate greenhouse gas emissions from motor vehicles, since emissions are clearly air pollutants under the Clean Air Act.[57]

Responding to the court decision, EPA on December 15, 2009, issued a finding that greenhouse gas emissions from motor vehicles endangered the public.[58] This finding supported the promulgation of new greenhouse gas emissions standards for new automobiles and light trucks on April 1, 2010. In 2001, the U.S. Supreme Court in *Whitman v. American Trucking Associations* unanimously issued an important decision pertaining to a factor the EPA may not consider in revising national airquality standards (NAQS) for ozone and particulate matter. The Court (1) upheld the delegation by the 1990 Clean Air Act Amendments of authority to the EPA to promulgate NAQS at a level "requisite to protect public health" against the charge the delegation was an unconstitutional delegation of legislative power, (2) opined the EPA may not take economic considerations into account when promulgating ambient standards under Section 109 of the Clean Air Act, (3) the EPA's policy for implementing its revised ozone NAQS in nonattainment areas was a final action subject to judicial review, (4) the 1990 amendments regarding ozone in nonattainment areas were ambiguous and therefore required deference to the EPA's interpretation, and (5) the EPA may not enforce its revised zone NAQS in a manner rendering the ozone specific Clean Air Act amendment ineffective.[59]

ACCOMPLISHMENTS

There is general agreement the Clean Air Act, as amended, has reduced substantially air pollution. Nevertheless, the promulgated EPA uniform national standards have been criticized on the ground that variations among the states have been authorized by the EPA and millions of persons live in nonattainment areas. Cass R. Sunstein in 1999 concluded, the "national standards have mostly served not as real law, but as a target or *aspirations*—flexible goals to which the federal government can point without, however, insisting on compliance unless or until it is reasonable."[60]

In 1999, the EPA released a report to Congress on its estimates of the benefits and costs of the Clean Air Act in the period 1990 to 2010.[61] The report concluded the amendments will reduce significantly emission of air pollutants in the period, compliance costs to attain and maintain national ambient air-quality standards will total $14.5 billion, and benefits will include reducing the incidence of a number of adverse health effects of pollutants, improved visibility, and avoidance of damage to agricultural products.

The U.S. Government Accountability Office in 2006 published a report revealing the EPA had completed 404 of the 452 actions it was required to initiate under Titles I, III, and IV of the Clean Air Act Amendments of 1990.[62] A total of 256 required actions to be completed by April 2005 were completed late, including 161 completed in two or fewer years after the specified date.

In 1997, the EPA released the results of two studies of the benefits and costs of the Clean Air Act: One study covered the period 1970 to 1990, and the other study covered the period 1990 to 2010.[63] The second study predicted emissions estimates for 2010 would be 39 percent lower than the pre-1990 estimates or a reduction of almost 11 million tons. The NO_2 emissions cap-and-trade program was credited for close to one-half of the reduction.

Alan Krupnick and Richard Morgenstern in 2002 reviewed the two studies and noted hazardous air pollutants emissions were "not extensively considered in either study," and changes in particulate matter and ozone ambient standards also were not considered in the 2010 study.[64] They concluded: "Subject to some methodological qualifications, the two Section 812 studies already completed indicate that the aggregate benefits of past and ongoing policies to improve air quality have clearly exceeded the costs incurred by industry, taxpayers, and consumers."[65]

Christopher T. Giovinazzo in 2003 reached a dramatic conclusion: "The Clean Air Act is a symbolic law: it cannot be read and implemented literally; EPA must inject pragmatism to rationalize CAA's otherwise absurd literal results."[66] In 2004, Michael Greenstone released the results of his econometric study to determine the reason(s) for the 80 percent decline in sulfur dioxide air pollution since the enactment of the Clean Air Act Amendments of 1970. He concluded: "The cause of the dramatic reduction in ambient SO_2 remains a mystery."[67] In his judgment, other provisions of the amendments or state and local government regulations may explain the decline.

William W. Buzbee reported in 2010, "many states have no interest in going beyond federal levels of protection and have enacted laws precluding such action."[68] He concluded, however, the Clean Air Act's "substantial reliance on cooperative federalism structures includes delegated programs, savings clause, and regulatory floors, all of which have facilitated experimentation and allowed state climate change leadership."[69]

Tom Tietenberg in 2010 noted "air quality has improved substantially under emissions trading. For some programs the degree to which credit for these improvements can be attributed solely to emissions trading (as opposed to exogenous factors of complementary polities) is not completely clear."[70]

The EPA reported in 2011 total emissions of carbon monoxide declined from approximately 204 million tons in 1970 to approximately 77 million tons in 2008.[71] There also was a decline from 31 million tons in 1970 to 11 million tons in 2008 of emissions of sulfur dioxide, with more than one-half of the decline attributable to the Clean Air Act Amendments *of 1990*. EPA Administrator Lisa P. Jackson testified in 2011 before a U.S. House of Representatives subcommittee that "programs implemented pursuant to the *Clean Air Act Amendments of 1990* are estimated to have saved over 160,000 lives, spared Americans more than 100,000 hospital visits, and prevented millions of cases of respiratory problems, including bronchitis and asthma."[72]

A 2011 EPA report revealed thirty-nine states have met the health-based national air-quality standards for lead, and "national average concentration of lead in the air have dropped 93 percent nationwide since 1980."[73] Craig N. Oren reached the following conclusion in 2010: "What we do need is not a new Act, but more vigorous implementation . . ."[74] The reader should be aware one of the most difficult air-quality problems to solve is ozone.

Douglas R. Williams in 2013 noted environmental regulatory laws are based on cooperative federalism, and opined: "This approach to environmental management is becoming strained and ineffective."[75] He suggested responsibility for environmental protection should be transferred from the EPA to federal regional environmental management agencies that would be "a promising alternative to our now outdated 1970s-vintage regulatory programs."[76]

SUMMARY AND CONCLUSIONS

The large geographical area of the United States and the diversity of conditions as well as the exceedingly large national deficit and large debt argue against Congress assuming complete control of air pollution abatement. State governments have experienced air-quality officers and the necessary equipment to operate abatement programs. The reader should note the regulatory program authorized by the Clean Air Act reduced state discretion in establishing programs to abate air pollution.

The regional greenhouse gas initiative demonstrates states cooperatively can launch and operate a successful program to solve an interstate environmental problem in the absence of preemptive congressional regulation designed to solve an interstate externalities problem such as air pollution.

Chapter 4 examines maximum state regulatory authority and regulatory authority turn-back statutes.

Chapter 4

Maximum State Regulatory Standards Statutes and Regulatory Authority Turn-Back Statutes

Congress enacted one innovative preemption statute forbidding subnational government regulatory standards to exceed the national maximum regulatory standards established by the statute. In addition, Congress enacted four complete preemption statutes and one partial preemption statute turning back very limited regulatory authority to states by allowing them to conduct inspections, provided federal inspection standards are used.

FEDERAL MAXIMUM STANDARDS

The insurance industry is of great interstate and international importance, yet the U.S Supreme Court in 1868 opined insurance was not commerce and consequently was exempt from congressional regulation.[1] The Court in 1944 reversed this decision.[2] The states, concerned with the loss of revenue flowing from the decision, successfully lobbied Congress to enact the McCarran-Ferguson Act of 1945 reversing the decision by devolving power to the states to regulate the insurance industry.[3] In consequence, nonuniform and often discriminatory state insurance regulatory policies persisted.

Insurance companies continued to challenge state discriminatory policies in court and also lobbied Congress for relief. Congress enacted the Gramm-Leach-Bliley Financial Modernization Act of 1999, the first comprehensive overhaul of federal financial regulation statutes since the enactment of major financial statutes in the 1930s.[4] This act placed a cap on the stringency of state insurance regulations in thirteen specified areas.

States may impose only restrictions substantially identical to and no more burdensome or restrictive than the below specified restrictions in the act:

(i) restrictions prohibiting the rejection of an insurance policy by a depository institution or an affiliate of a depository institution solely because the policy has been issued or underwritten by any person who is not associated with such depository institution or affiliate when the insurance is required in connection with a loan or extension of credit . . . ;

(ii) restrictions prohibiting a requirement for any debtor, insurer, or insurance agent or broker to pay a separate charge in connection with the handling of insurance that is required in connection with a loan or other extension of credit or the provisions of another traditional banking product by a depository institution unless such charge would be required when the depository institution or affiliate is the licensed insurance agent or broker providing the insurance;

(iii) restrictions prohibiting the use of any advertisement or other insurance promotional materials by a depository institution that would cause a reasonable person to believe mistakenly that

(1) the federal government or a state is responsible for the insurance sales activities of, or standards behind the credit of, the institution or affiliate; or

(2) a state or the federal government guarantees any returns on insurance products or is a source of payments on any insurance obligation sold by the institution or affiliate;

(iv) restrictions prohibiting the payment or receipt of any commission or brokerage fee or other valuable consideration for services as an insurance agent or broker to or by any persons, unless such persons holds a valid state license regarding the applicable class of insurance at the time at which the services are performed, except that, in this clause, the term "services as an insurance agent or broker" does not include referral by an unlicensed person or a customer or potential customer to a license insurance agent or broker that does not include a discussion of specific insurance policy terms and conditions;

(v) restrictions prohibiting any compensation paid to or received by an individual who is not licensed to sell insurance for the referral of a customer that seeks to purchase, or seeks an opinion or advice on, any insurance product to a person that sells or provides opinions or advice on such product, based on the purchase of insurance by the customer . . . ;

(vi) restrictions prohibiting the use of health information obtained from the insurance records of a customer for any purpose other than for its activities as a licensed agent or broker without the express consent of the customer;

(vii) restrictions prohibiting the use of health information obtained from the insurance records of a customer for any purpose other than for its activities as a licensed agent or broker without the express consent of the customer . . .

(viii) restrictions prohibiting the extension of credit or any product or service that is equivalent to an extension of credit, lease or sale of property of any kind, or furnishing of any services or fixing or varying the consideration for any of the foregoing, on the condition or requirement that the customer obtain insurance from a depository institution or an affiliate of a depository institution, or a particular insurer, agent, or broker, other than a prohibition that would prevent any such depository institution or affiliate—

(1) from engaging in any activity described in this clause that would not violate section 106 of the *Bank Holding Company Act Amendments of 1970* as interpreted by the Board of Governors of the Federal Reserve System, or

(2) from informing a customer or prospective customer that insurance is required to obtain a loan or credit, that loan or credit approval is contingent on the procurement by the customer of acceptable insurance, or that insurance is available from the depository institution or affiliate of the depository institution;

(ix) restrictions requiring, when an application by a customer for a loan or other extension of credit from a depository institution is pending, and insurance is offered or sold to the consumer or is required in connection with the loan or extension of credit by the depository institution or any affiliate thereof, that written disclosure be provided to the customer or prospective customer indicating that the customer's choice of an insurance provider will not affect the credit decision or credit terms in any way, except that the depository institution may impose reasonable requirements concerning the creditworthiness of the insurer and scope of coverage chosen;

(x) restrictions requiring clear and conspicuous disclosure, in writing, where practicable, to the customer prior to the sale of any insurance policy that such policy—

(I) is not a deposit;

(II) is not insured by the FDIC;

(III) is not guaranteed by any depository institution or, if appropriate, an affiliate of any such institution or any person soliciting the purchase of or selling insurance on the premises thereof; and

(IV) where appropriate, involves investment risk, including potential loss of principal.

(xi) restrictions requiring that, when a customer obtained insurance (other than credit insurance or flood insurance) and credit from a depository institution, or any affiliate of such institution, or any person soliciting the purchase of or selling Insurance on the premises thereof, the credit and insurance transactions be completed through separate documents.

(xii) restrictions prohibiting, when a customer obtains insurance (other than credit insurance or flood insurance) and credit from a depository institution or an affiliate of such institution, or any person soliciting the purchase of or selling insurance on the premises thereof, inclusion of the expense of insurance premiums in the primary credit transaction without the express written consent of the customer; and

(xiii) restrictions requiring maintenance of separate and distinct books and records relating to insurance transactions, including all files relating to and reflecting consumer complaints, and requiring that such insurance books and records be made available to the appropriate state insurance regulator for inspection on reasonable notice.

The act also contains a contingent preemption provision providing a federal insurance agent licensing system will be implemented if twenty-six state legislatures do not enact by November 12, 2002, a uniform licensing system for agents to be determined by the National Association of Insurance Commissioners (NAIC) after consulting state insurance commissioners.[5] The NAIC, on September 10, 2002, certified that thirty-five state legislatures had enacted statutes establishing such a system.[6] The NAIC also drafted and promoted the enactment by forty-seven state legislatures of a Producer Licensing Model Act providing for interstate reciprocity.[7]

State insurance commissioners, working through their association, promoted uniform state policies and launched an accreditation program involving an independent team reviewing the policies of each state insurance department to determine its compliance with the standards.[8] The U.S. General Accounting Office reported the association "through its accreditation program had made considerable progress in achieving greater uniformity in carrying out their financial solvency oversight responsibilities."[9] The NAIC drafted an interstate insurance compact, enacted by forty-four states, establishing uniform regulatory policies for annuity, disability income, life, and long-term health care products.

COOPERATIVE ENFORCEMENT

To date, Congress has enacted four otherwise complete preemption statutes returning limited regulatory authority to states. In addition, Congress authorized states to cooperate in the enforcement of four federal regulatory programs, and enacted twenty-one statutes devolving authority to state attorneys general to enforce specified congressional preemption acts.

REGULATORY AUTHORITY TURN-BACKS

Congress on four occasions amended a complete preemption statute to authorize a department head or agency administrator to return specified regulatory authority to states submitting applications for such a return.

Low-Level Atomic Energy. The Atomic Energy Act of 1946 is a complete preemption act removing from state and local governments all authority to regulate ionizing radiation.[10] Congress amended the act in 1954 to authorize private development and use of atomic energy, and thereby immediately necessitated preparatory actions by state governments and by local governments to ensure the safety of citizens, including evacuation of all people within a specified distance of a nuclear electric generating station.[11] The planning board and the city council would have to review zoning regulations to determine the areas where use of ionizing radiation would be safe.[12] Safety considerations necessitated initiation by municipalities of specialized programs to train and equip several departments to respond to incidents involving radioactive materials. Particularly affected are the building, fire, health, police, and water departments.[13] The school department also would be called upon to provide education on radioactive materials and precautions to be taken against radiation burns.

The 1946 act was amended in 1959 to authorize the Atomic Energy Commission (now Nuclear Regulatory Commission) to enter into agreements with states, permitting them to assume specified regulatory responsibilities for low-level atomic energy.[14] A state radiation control program must be compatible with, but not necessarily identical to, the Nuclear Regulatory Commission's regulatory program.

Grain Inspection. Foreign complaints about the quality of grains exported from the United States persuaded Congress to grant the U.S. Department of Agriculture complete responsibility for official inspections and weighing of all grains. In 1968, however, Congress decided to devolve power to state agencies to perform official inspection and weighing in accordance with national standards.[15]

Railroad Inspection. Frequent railroad accidents persuaded Congress that the U.S. government should be responsible for safety inspections of all railroad equipment. However, Congress in 1970 recognized that states could conduct quality safety inspections of motor vehicles and should be permitted to conduct railroad equipment inspections on a voluntary basis. In consequence, Congress enacted the Federal Railroad Safety Act of 1970, authorizing voluntary state inspections of railroad equipment and facilities in accordance with national standards, thereby shifting some of the inspection costs to the participating states.[16]

Hazardous and Solid Wastes. In 1976, Congress enacted the Hazardous Materials Transportation Act Amendments that assigned the U.S. Environmental Protection Agency partial responsibility for regulating the transportation of hazardous wastes.[17] In 1984, Congress enacted the Hazardous and Solid Waste Amendments permitting states to assume responsibility for the EPA's hazardous waste program.[18] Currently, all states have assumed responsibility for the initial or basic program, and many states have assumed responsibility for other parts of the program, including land disposal restrictions.

Cooperative Enforcement. The Age Discrimination in Employment Amendments of 1986 authorizes the U.S. Equal Employment Opportunity Commission to sign cooperative enforcement agreements with state and local governments fair employment agencies.[19]

The Oil Pollution Act of 1990 grants authority to states to enforce on their respective navigable waters only "the requirements for evidence of financial responsibility" of the party responsible for a ship transporting oil as cargo or fuel.[20]

The Anti Car Theft Act of 1992, a complete preemption act, directs the U.S. Attorney General and U.S. attorneys "to work with State and local officials to investigate car thefts, including . . . armed carjacking . . ."[21]

The Antiterrorism and Effective Death Penalty Act of 1996 authorizes state and local government law enforcement officers to arrest an illegal alien or a person convicted of a felony in the United States, who was deported or left the country after conviction subject to obtaining information from the Immigration and Naturalization Service on the status of such a person.[22]

The Coast Guard and Maritime Transportation Act of 2004 grants authority to state and local government law enforcement officers to enforce state criminal laws by arresting persons for violating a federal security zone regulation.[23]

The Magnuson-Stevens Fishery Conservation and Management Reauthorization Act of 2006 allows a governor to request the Secretary of the Interior to execute a joint enforcement agreement authorizing "the deputization and funding of state law enforcement officers with marine law enforcement responsibilities to perform" the secretary's law enforcement duties.[24]

Authorization of State Lawsuits. Each of the following fifteen complete congressional statutes devolves authority to state attorneys general to bring suits in court to enforce congressional statutes.

The Nutrition Labeling and Education Act of 1920 grants a state attorney general authority to bring proceedings for the civil enforcement or to restrain violations of specified sections of the act provided "the food that is the subject of the proceedings is located in the State."[25]

The Federal Environmental Pesticide Control Act of 1972 authorizes the EPA administrator to enter into cooperative enforcement agreements with state attorneys general and to make grants to states to cover part of their enforcement costs.[26]

The Consumer Product Safety Improvement Act of 1990 amends the Hazardous Substances Act and the Flammable Fabrics Act by authorizing a state attorney general to bring a civil action for an injunction to enforce the acts.[27]

The Oil Pollution Act of 1990 authorizes a state to enforce on its navigable waters the federal requirements for evidence of financial responsibility.[28]

The Telephone Consumer Protection Act of 1991 grants authority to a state attorney general to bring a civil action on behalf of state residents against any person violating the act and regulations promulgated under its authority.[29]

Congress enacted a partial preemption act, the Telephone Disclosure and Dispute Resolution Act of 1992, devolving authority on a state attorney general to bring a civil action on behalf of his or her citizens in the U.S. District Court to enforce compliance with rules and regulations promulgated under the act by the Federal Communication Commission.[30]

The Telemarketing and Consumer Fraud and Abuse Prevention Act of 1994, a complete preemption statute, authorizes each state, as *parens patriae*, to "bring a civil suit in an appropriate District Court of the United States to enjoin such telemarketing, to enforce compliance with such rule of the [federal communications] commission, to obtain damages, restitution, or other compensation on behalf of" its residents.[31]

The Capital Markets Efficiency Act of 1996, contained in the National Securities Markets Improvement Act of 1996, devolves enforcement authority upon states: "Consistent with this section, the securities commission (or any other office performing like functions) of any State shall retain jurisdiction under the laws of such State to investigate and bring enforcement actions with respect to fraud or deceit, or unlawful conduct by a broker or dealer, in connection with securities or securities transactions."[32]

The Consumer Credit Reporting Reform Act of 1996 devolves authority to each state attorney general to bring an action in the U.S.

District Court to enjoin a violation of the act, and also exempts from preemption any state law "relating to the prescreening of consumer reports" and other specified state laws in effect in 1996, including section 54A(a) of chapter 93 of the Massachusetts Annotated Laws . . ."[33]

The Omnibus Consolidated Appropriations Act for Fiscal Year 1996 amends the *Fair Credit Reporting Act* by allowing a state attorney general to bring an enforcement action against any person violating the act and to seek damages.[34]

The Children Online Privacy Protection Act of 1998 grants each state attorney general authority to bring a *parens patriae* civil suit in the U.S. District Court if he or she believes "an interest of the residents of that state has been or is threatened, or adversely affected by the engagement of any person in a practice that violates any regulations of the commission" (Federal Trade Commission).[35]

The Twenty-First Amendment Enforcement Act of 2000 authorizes a state attorney general to bring a civil action for injunctive relief in the U.S. District Court to restrain an individual believed to be violating a state law regulating the importation of intoxicating liquor into the state and to enforce compliance with the law.[36]

The Controlling the Assault of Non-Solicited Pornography and Marketing Act of 2003 authorizes state attorneys general to bring a civil suit to protect their respective state against residents who have been or are "threatened or adversely affected" by an individual who violates the act.[37]

The Junk Fax Prevention Act of 2005 similarly grants authority to state attorneys general to bring a civil suit in the U.S. District Court to enjoin unsolicited messages.[38]

The Restore Online Shoppers Confidence Act of 2010 authorizes a state attorney general or other state officer to "bring an action on behalf of state residents in any U.S. District Court in which the defendant is found, resides, or transacts business, or wherever venue is proper under section 1391 of title 28, United States Code, to obtain appropriate injunctive relief."[39]

SUMMMARY

Congress authorized states to assist in the enforcement of specified preemption statutes, and also enacted the Gramm-Leach-Bliley Finance Modernization Act of 1999, restricting the stringency of state insurance regulations in thirteen specified areas. Cooperative federalism is still alive as revealed by four statutes returning limited regulatory authority to states, and twenty-one statutes devolving authority upon state attorneys general to file lawsuits to enforce federal statutes. These and other congressional statutes have contributed to important changes in governance in the U.S. federal system.

Chapter 5 is devoted to state-friendly preemption statutes, including one complete preemption statute.

Chapter 5

State-Friendly Preemption Statutes

The interstate commerce clause of the U.S. Constitution grants broad powers to Congress to regulate commerce among the several states. The clause frequently has been employed to remove completely or partially regulatory powers from state governments and local governments, and to impose mandates and restraints upon them.[1] Subnational governments welcome certain preemption statutes, because they are of assistance to these governmental units. This chapter focuses upon innovative state-friendly preemption statutes.

INNOVATIVE STATUTES

Congress enacted the Johnson Act of 1951, making it unlawful for any person to transport a gambling device into a state, but included an "opt-out" provision allowing a state legislature to enact a law stipulating the act's prohibition does not "apply to any gambling device used or designed for use at or transported to licensed gambling establishments where betting is legal under applicable laws."[2]

The twenty-eight minimum-standards preemption acts date to the Water Quality Act of 1965, and are state-friendly, as their purpose is to ensure only state governments are responsible for regulating specific fields, provided their standards meet or exceed the national standards and are enforced (see chapter 2).

The Coastal Zone Management Act of 1972 and the Nuclear Waste Policy Act of 1982 are partial preemption statutes authorizing a state veto of a decision by a U.S. department or agency subject to an override of the veto by the U.S. Secretary of Commerce and Congress, respectively.[3] The acts, in effect, offer a degree of protection against federal government administrators by subjecting their decisions to a mandated review.

The former act is an unusually state-friendly one, as it stipulates a state coastal zone management program approved by the Secretary of Commerce prohibits a federal department or agency to issue a license or permit to a private applicant to undertake an activity if the concerned state objects to the application. The act provides for a reverse type of preemption subject to an override by the secretary.

Congress in enacting the Toxic Substances Control Act of 1976 accorded states a degree of regulatory flexibility by empowering them to continue to regulate a chemical mixture and substance until the Environmental Protection Agency Administrator promulgates a rule applicable to the mixture or substances.[4] The act also provides the administrator in promulgating that a rule may exempt the concerned mixture or substance from the rule if state regulations do not place an undue burden on interstate commerce and offer a higher degree of public protection.

A second reverse-preemption section is contained in the Port and Tanker Safety Act of 1978, and preempts the requirement for federally licensed pilots on tankers engaged in foreign commerce in navigable waters when a state legislature enacts a statute mandating state-licensed pilots on such tankers and notifies the Secretary of Transportation.[5]

A state governor or a state legislature is empowered by the Nuclear Waste Policy Act of 1982 to veto a site for a high-level radioactive waste facility selected by the Secretary of Energy.[6] Congress in 1987 nullified this innovative procedure by eliminating two of the three identified sites subject to further tests of the Yucca Mountain site in Nevada by the Department of Energy.[7] Congress formally overrode the notice of disapproval of the Yucca Mountain site submitted by the governor of Nevada on April 8, 2002.[8]

The Coast Guard Authorization Act of 1984 directs the U.S. secretary of Transportation to develop standards for determining whether a marine recreational vessel operator is intoxicated.[9] The Coast Guard, now a unit of the Department of Homeland Security, promulgated in 1987 a rule stipulating a state blood-alcohol content (BAC) standard, if one exist, is the national standard within the state. In consequence, the national standard (currently 00.8 percent BAC) applies only in states lacking a state BAC standard.

As noted in chapter 3, Congress in 1986 amended the Atlantic Striped Bass Conservation Act by including a contingent provision directing states to comply with the management plans developed by the Atlantic States Marine Fisheries Commission.[10]

The Abandoned Shipwreck Act of 1987, a complete preemption act, is a state-friendly one asserting a federal government title to each such shipwreck and directing the transfer of the title to the state in whose waters the shipwreck is located.[11]

The Riegle-Neal Interstate Banking and Branching Efficiency Act of 1994 contains an "opt-out" section authorizing a state legislature to enact a statute prohibiting interstate branching within the state otherwise authorized by the act.[12] The act also contains an "opt-in" section allowing a state legislature to permit interstate branching through *de novo* branches provided the state law "applies equally to all banks, and expressly permits all out-of-state banks to establish *de novo* branches" in the state.[13]

Congress in 1994 revised, recodified, and added a new section to the transportation statutes, effective September 30, 1996, stipulating a state "may establish, maintain, or enforce a law or regulation that has a fuel use tax reporting requirement (including any tax reporting form) only if the requirement conforms with the International Fuel Tax Agreement."[14] This section respects state sovereignty because the agreement was developed and may be revised by states and Canadian provinces.[15]

Congress enacted the Electronic Signatures in Global and National Commerce Act of 2000, which preempted completely forty-four state digital signatures laws with respect to interstate and foreign commerce, but exempts from preemption any state statute or rule constituting "an enactment or adoption of the Uniform Electronic Transaction Act as approved and recommended for enactment in all the States by the National Conference of Commissioners on Uniform State Laws."[16] This section also respects state sovereignty.

Two nongrant and nonpreemptive congressional statutes promote uniform regulation by states. The Hotel and Motel Fire Safety Act of 1990 is designed to encourage states to adopt federal standards by stipulating federal government officers and employees may stay only in facilities meeting the safety standards specified by the Federal Fire Prevention and Control Act of 1974.[17] Each state governor is authorized to provide the U.S. Administrator of General Services with a list of hotels and motels meeting the federal fire safety standards. Furthermore, federal conditional grants-in-aid to subnational governments may not be used to sponsor or to pay for a conference, convention, meeting, or training seminar in a hotel or motel failing to meet the national fire safety standards.

The Muhammad Ali Boxing Reform Act of 2000 seeks:

(1) to protect the rights and welfare of professional boxers on an interstate basis by preventing certain exploitive, oppressive, and unethical business practices;

(2) to assist State boxing commissioners in their efforts to provide more effective public oversight of the sport; and

(3) to promote honorable competition in professional boxing and enhance the overall integrity of the industry.[18]

The act directs the association of state boxing commissions, by a majority vote of its member state boxing commissioners, must adopt "guidelines for objective and consistent written criteria for the ratings of professional boxers."[19] In lieu of mandating the commissions to follow the guidelines, the act simply provides it is "the sense of Congress" the guidelines should be followed.[20]

RECOMMENDATIONS

Congress should continue to employ the innovative approaches described above where appropriate, and to draft and enact statutes uniting the resources of the national government and the state governments in a campaign to solve major problems, as suggested in 1925 by Felix Frankfurter and James M. Landis, who noted state legislatures and Congress interact with each other even though their respective fields of authority have not been delimited clearly and added:

In as much as there are two categories of law-making agencies, State and Nation, the solution of the problem has usually been conceived in terms of exclusive duality. Evils calling for legislative redress, recognized subjects of administrative control, governmental promotion of social ends, have . . . divided men into two hostile camps, those seeking relief through State legal inventiveness and those appealing for national intervention. As a result legal inventiveness has been curbed and its resources largely confined to an untrue antithesis. The combined legislative powers of Congress and the several States permit a wide range of permutations and combinations for governmental action. Until very recently these potentialities have been left largely unexplored.[21]

Frankfurter and Landis were referring to the great potential of interstate compacts to solve major regional and national problems. Although they did not specifically suggest the possibility of federal-interstate compacts, it is apparent these compacts are an example of what they had in mind. Currently, there are seven federal-state compacts combining the resources of the national governments and states: Delaware River Basin Compact, Appalachian Regional Compact, Susquehanna River Basin Compact, Apalachicola-Chattahoochee-Flint River Basins Compacts, Interstate Agreement on Detainers, National Crime Prevention and Privacy Compact, and Alabama-Coosa-Tallapoosa Rivers Basins Compacts.[22]

We conclude Congress and state legislatures should take the lead in developing and promoting additional federal-interstate compacts, and federal-state administrative agreements that may cover the same subjects as federal-interstate compacts.

SUMMARY AND CONCLUSIONS

The acts described in this chapter collectively produced a revolution in national-state relations and are evidence the theory of cooperative federalism is not outdated, although it is in need of supplementation by a broader theory of United States federalism. The experience of the seven federal-interstate compacts is evidence that legal approaches combining the resources of the national government are successful in solving what had been intractable problems.

Chapter 6

Contingent Preemption Statutes

The year 1965 witnessed the appearance of two new types of innovative preemption statutes: minimum national standards statutes, described in chapter 2, and contingent preemption statutes that become applicable to a state government or a local government only if one or two specified conditions prevail within the government. This approach is similar to the classical sword of Damocles or the gun behind the door approach.

James Madison feared state legislatures might enact statutes harmful to the proposed union of states if they were allowed to enact statutes without approval by the proposed Congress. He argued at the constitutional convention in 1787 in favor of a national negative applicable to state statutes:

> The necessity of a general government proceeds from the propensity of the states to pursue their particular interests in opposition to the general interest. This propensity will continue to disturb the system, unless effectively controlled. Nothing short of a negative on their laws will control it. They can pass laws which will accomplish their injurious objects before they can be repealed by the General Legislature or be set aside by the national tribunals. . . . Its utility is sufficiently displayed in the British system. Nothing could maintain the harmony and subordination of the various parts of the empire, but the prerogative by which the Crown stifles in the birth every act of every part tending to discord or encroachment.[1]

The convention rejected his proposal, in part because review of state laws by the proposed Congress would prevent the implementation of state laws approved by Congress for a year or more after their enactment because of the slow pace of communications. The rejection of his proposal, of course, meant state legislatures would be free to encroach upon the powers of the general government, but the encroaching laws would be subject to the Constitution's supremacy of the law clause and could be invalided by courts.

The subject of national government review of state laws prior to their effective date was raised again in the 1960s, as numerous black citizens in southern states were prevented from voting in primary elections and/or general elections. State ratification of the Fifteenth Amendment to the United States Constitution in 1870 granted broad powers to Congress to guarantee the right of U.S. citizens to vote may not be abridged or denied "by the United States or by any State on account of race, color, or previous condition of servitude."

CONTINGENT PREEMPTION

The U.S. Constitution grants important regulatory powers to Congress, including those contained in the Fifteenth Amendment. Congress for the first time employed its preemption powers in 1790, when it enacted the Copyright Act and the Patent Act completely removing from states authority to regulate copyrights and patents.[2] Congress enacted preemption statutes at a slow pace and only 29 such statutes were enacted prior to 1900. The pace of enactment continued to be relatively slow until the mid-1960s, but increased sharply thereafter with the total reaching 705 statutes by June 2015.

Preemption statutes, as explained in chapter 2, can be complete, partial, or contingent. This chapter focuses on contingent preemption statutes. The first such statute is the Voting Rights Act of 1965, and it is the most important contingent preemption statute.[3] Congress subsequently enacted three preemption acts with each containing a contingent provision: Atlantic Striped Bass Conservation Act Amendments of 1986, Gramm-Leach-Bliley Financial Modernization Act of 1999, and Energy Policy Act of 2005.[4]

VOTING RIGHTS ACT OF 1965

State ratification of the Fifteenth Amendment granted Congress unlimited authority to enact statutes to protect the voting rights of black citizens, including congressional use of the veto power to disallow state election laws denying or hindering the exercise of the right to vote of black citizens. Congress in 1965 enacted a statute, based on the sword of Damocles approach, to guarantee the voting rights of these citizens in the form of two conditions whose presence in a state or local government triggers the application of the act to the concerned government.[5] The conditions are the employment of a test or device to abridge the rights of citizens to vote because of race or color as of November 1, 1964, and fewer than 50 percent of persons of voting age cast ballots in the 1964 presidential election. The act later was amended to stipulate fewer than 50 percent of voting age cast ballots in the 1964, 1968, or 1972 presidential election.

A governmental unit covered by the act automatically becomes subject to the act's Section 5 preclearance requirement prohibiting any change, no matter how major or minor, in its election system unless the United States attorney general, within sixty days of submission of a proposed change to him or her, fails to register an objection. Alternatively, the concerned government may seek a declaratory judgment by the U.S. District Court for the District of Columbia holding the proposed change(s) will not abridge the right to vote of the protected citizens.

The Voting Rights Act Amendments of 1975, citing the powers granted to Congress by the Fourteenth Amendment to enforce its guarantees, expanded the act's coverage to include language minorities defined as "persons who are American-Indian, Asian American, Alaska Natives, or of Spanish heritage."[6] Amendments to the act in 1992 require each covered jurisdiction to provide bilingual voting materials if any protected language minority constitutes 5 percent or more of the voting-age population of a governmental unit and less than one-half of these voters cast ballots in one of the specified presidential elections.[7] The act also applies to a governmental unit if more than 5 percent of the citizens are members of one language minority group and the group's illiteracy rate exceeds the national illiteracy rate.

The concerned federal authorities will not approve a requested change(s) in a covered governmental unit's voting system until they are satisfied the right of racial and foreign language minorities to participate in the electoral process is safeguarded. As the result of the legal standards formulated to protect the voting rights of these minorities, a trend toward federal imposition of the single-member district—or ward—electoral system is discernible. The U.S. Supreme Court's preference for this system is implicit in many of the Court's racial discrimination decisions.[8]

These decisions allowed lawsuits seeking the replacement of at-large voting systems, thus reversing the previously widespread transformation from the ward system to the at-large system promoted by the municipal reform movement and the progressive movement to remove corruption from cities, and to ensure council decisions were based upon citywide needs and not political patronage.[9]

The U.S. Supreme Court in *Shelby County, Alabama v. Holder* in 2013 struck down as unconstitutional the Voting Rights Act provision setting forth its coverage formula by opining "the conditions that originally justified these measures no longer characterize voting conditions in covered jurisdictions."[10]

HISTORICAL BACKGROUND

Many municipalities during the nineteenth century patterned their government structures after those existing at the national and state levels, and adopted large bicameral councils elected under the ward system. A movement to reform city governments gathered momentum in the 1890s as the problems, including corruption, created by political machines and the increasing complexities of municipal life proved difficult to correct under the existing ward systems. The municipal reform movement strongly attacked the ward system, and identified several major deficiencies. The system confined each voter's influence to his or her particular ward or election district, and ward representatives naturally attempted to win favor with their electorate by persuading the city council to grant benefits to their respective ward, regardless of the ultimate effect of the council's actions on the city as a whole.

Because each voter's interest primarily extended to that portion of the political process with which he or she had some influence, the politics of any given ward generally interested only its residents. Thus, self-serving political cliques developed in relative obscurity within wards, free from close scrutiny by the press or the general public. Another major problem aggravated by the ward system was inequality in representation. As a consequence of either deliberate gerrymandering or gradual population shifts, ward boundaries often favored a political faction of the population. These factions frequently acquired a disproportionate control of the city council and were able to resist redistricting for extended time periods. The demise of the ward system in many municipalities has been attributed primarily to these factors. [11]

The three major goals of the municipal reform movement were the elimination of municipal corruption, the achievement of increased efficiency and economy in the provision of municipal services, and the attainment of improved representation in municipal government. Convinced a positive correction existed between the electoral system and the responsiveness of the governing body to its citizens, the reform movement's participants sought changes in the electoral system and a reduction in the size of the city council. The reformers urged the replacement of partisan elections, the ward electoral system, and a large bicameral city council with a small unicameral council elected at-large by non-partisan ballots.[12]

An at-large electoral system presumably would correct several deficiencies perceived in the ward electoral system. Thus, council members would be encouraged to perceive problems in terms of their impact on the city as a whole. Moreover, neither deliberate nor inadvertent inequities in numerical apportionment could arise because elections would be citywide and each voter would make his or her selections from an identical list of candidates. By downgrading the political cliques' influence in the election of councilors, the elimination of wards as electoral districts also would discourage the development of the small-scale organizations so important to the political machines' ability to maintain their power.

Numerous municipalities adopted the at-large system as a result of the municipal reform movement, and many students of local government believe the reform program improved the quality of municipal government. More recent developments, however, necessitated a reassessment of the electoral system promoted by the reformers. A major objection to the use of at-large elections is that the system permits the overrepresentation of a cohesive majority, such as middle-class white voters, thereby denying any direct representation to a sizable minority group(s). For example, blacks in Albany, Georgia, who constituted 40 percent of the city's population at the time of the enactment of the Voting Rights Act of 1965, were unable to elect a single black citizen to any elective office in that city for over twenty-five years under the at-large system. Such disproportionate representation may create or aggravate minority-group alienation and feelings of political impotence, which eventually may lead to a complete withdrawal by these citizens from participation in the political process. A ruling white majority under an at-large electoral system may maintain its overrepresented status, and may dilute the voting strength of a growing black minority by annexing a predominately white area. The results of such an annexation could transform a black majority within the city's original boundaries to a minority within the new city limits.

The representational inequitable problems created by at-large electoral systems compelled the U.S. Department of Justice, acting under authority of the Voting Rights Act of 1965, to direct the restructuring of many local electoral systems to protect the voting rights of black voters. Pursuant to this intervention, numerous at-large electoral systems have been replaced by the somewhat racially balanced single-member district electoral scheme in a reversal of the municipal reform movement's evolution away from that system.[13]

Many historical evils associated with the ward system have not reappeared in the modern era, but the use of the single-member district system to help a racial minority introduced some other significant sociopolitical inequities. An illustrative example involved the Hasidic Jews of Brooklyn.

THE HASIDIC JEWS

Congress specifically designed the *Voting Rights Act of 1965* to end voting discrimination in several southern states, but in 1970 the U.S. Attorney General determined three counties in New York were subject to the act as amended that year.[14] New York, in 1971, sought a declaratory judgment from the District Court for the District of Columbia, exempting the three counties from the act's coverage. With the approval of the U.S. Department of Justice, the court granted the judgment. The court had denied a motion to intervene made by the National Association for the Advancement of Colored People (NAACP) that appealed the ruling, without success, to the U.S. Supreme Court.[15] On remand, however, the NAACP's motion was granted by the District Court and, after reopening the declaratory judgment, NAACP obtained an order from the court holding the act as amended applied to congressional and legislative districts in Manhattan, Brooklyn, and the Bronx. The U.S. Supreme Court confirmed this decision, dismissing New York's arguments that U.S. Bureau of the Census population data, used by the attorney general in his determination that the act applied to these subdivisions, included 250,000 aliens of voting age who were ineligible to vote and that more than 50 percent of the electorate had voted.[16]

After failing to obtain an exemption from the act's coverage, a special session of the New York State Legislature was called in 1974 to redistrict the pertinent areas. The legislature was informed by the Voting Rights Section of the U.S. Department of Justice that the redistricting plan would not be approved unless it included specified districts redrawn to achieve a 65 percent black majority. Although the redistricting did not alter the total number of districts with nonwhite majorities, it increased the majority percentage of nonwhite residents in two Senate districts and in two Assembly districts, and decreased the nonwhite majority percentage in one Senate district and two Assembly districts.[17]

Representatives of Brooklyn's Hasidic Jews filed suit against the redistricting, and advanced arguments in the U.S. District Court by contending the new Assembly districts divided the Hasidic community, thus making it the victim of racial gerrymandering and diluting the value of the Hasidic Jews' votes, in violation of the Fourteenth Amendment's equal protection of the law and due process of law clauses.[18] The Hasidic community also challenged the assumption only black legislators could represent properly the interests of black citizens. In court testimony, Richard S. Scolaro, executive director of the legislative committee that drew the district boundaries, stated the Hasidic community was split between two Assembly districts solely because the U.S. Department of Justice insisted on a nonwhite majority in those districts.[19] Nevertheless, while the case was pending, the U.S. attorney general approved the new districts, dismissing objections made by Hasidic, Irish, Italian, and Polish groups on the ground the act was designed to prevent voting discrimination only on the basis of race or color, not on the basis of ethnic origin or religious belief.[20] The attorney general stressed his function under the act is not to dictate to New York a specific redistricting plan but, rather, to determine whether the scheme devised by the state was acceptable.[21]

The U.S. District Court similarly dismissed the Hasidic Jews' complaint, concluding the members of the community were not disenfranchised, and a state validly could consider race when redistricting to correct previous racial discrimination.[22] Affirming the lower court's decision, the U.S. Court of Appeals for the District of Columbia Circuit reasoned the redistricting did not cause the underrepresentation of whites, who comprised 65 percent of the population, inasmuch as approximately 70 percent of the Assembly and Senate districts in Kings County would contain white majorities.[23] The Court of Appeals was convinced a legislature would confront an impossible task if "a state must in a reapportionment draw lines so as to preserve ethnic community unity."[24]

In *United Jewish Organization, Incorporated v. Wilson*, the U.S. Supreme Court affirmed the U.S. Court of Appeal's decision by a seven-to-one margin.[25] The Supreme Court noted neither the Fourteenth Amendment nor the Fifteenth Amendment mandates a per se rule against using racial factors in districting and apportionment, and held the remedial nature of the Voting Rights Act permitted, and perhaps required, the use of racial considerations in reapportionments subject to the act.[26] Moreover, the Court maintained the Hasidic community was represented properly insofar as race was concerned, because the total portion of districts with white majorities corresponded closely to the total proportion of whites in the municipal population. In his partial concurrence, Justice William Brennan seemed to reflect the overall attitude of the majority when he indicated that although the redistricting unfortunately split the Hasidic community, that harm was outweighed by the benefit of ensuring nonwhite representation.[27]

This decision is disturbing for several major reasons. The Court's 1960 decision in *Gomillion v. Lightfoot* invalidated racial gerrymandering.[28] Furthermore, the Court ignored the wisdom in Justice William Douglas's dissent in *Wright v. Rockefeller*: "When racial or religious lines are drawn by the State, the multiracial, multi-religious communities that our Constitution seeks to weld together as one become separatist; antagonisms that relate to race or to religious rather than to political issues are generated, communities seek not the best representative but the best racial or religious partisan. Since that system is at war with the democratic ideal, it should find no footing here."[29]

Chief Justice Warren Burger, in his well-reasoned dissent in the *Hasidic Jews* decision, expressed concerns similar to those troubling Justice William Douglas and also noted the court's opinion could promote segregation by encouraging minorities to move into enclaves from where they could accumulate enough votes to elect a particular representative.[30] The chief justice correctly observed "the assumption that 'whites' and 'non-whites' in the County form homogeneous entities for voting purposes is entirely without foundation."[31] Thus, the legislators' description of Puerto Ricans as nonwhites when calculating the nonwhite majorities in the legislative districts was made under the erroneous assumption that blacks and Puerto Ricans in New York City have identical interests.[32]

The *Hasidic Jews* decision also must be criticized for condoning the institutionalized denial of the right to vote to the entire white minority in the 65 percent nonwhite districts. The court's conclusion the white minority had not been injured because the total percentage of districts with white majorities corresponded to the total percentage of whites in the county cannot be credited.[33] As Justice Brennan noted, the Hasidic Jews raised a question concerning their personal rights, not those of whites in general.[34] The court's majority unsatisfactory response to the question was the Hasidic community had no intrinsic right to select its own representative, and individual voters had no constitutional complaint if their candidate fails to win. Such an argument could be applied as easily to nonwhites who are unable to elect a particular representative because they are dispersed among many districts.[35] The Court's observations similarly could justify a conversion from a single-member district scheme to an at-large system in which a nonwhite minority never could elect their own representatives.

The most disturbing fact noted by Chief Justice Burger in his dissent was his comment the Hasidic community had been "carved up" for the sole purpose of racial gerrymandering.[36] In his opinion for the Court, Justice White agreed the purpose of creating a 65 percent nonwhite majority was "to ensure the opportunity for the election of a black representative."[37] The primary objective of the percentage requirements, therefore, was to render ineffective the white minority's participation in the election process in the event of racial block-voting.

Although this result may be legally permissible as a remedial measure within the scope of the Voting Rights Act, the result has imposed an extremely harsh burden on those ethnic and religious minorities who, in effect, are denied the right to cast an effective ballot. The imposition of such a system, even for the purpose of remedying past discrimination, should be avoided if a less severe alternative is available. The most conspicuous deficiency in Chief Justice Burger's dissent is the lack of a proposed alternative to the use of single-member districts that would avoid "unnecessary bias for or against any racial, ethnic, or religious group," and would comply with the Voting Rights Act.[38] Indeed, one primary objection to the Court's reaffirmation of the single-member district system, despite its harmful social effects, is that the electoral scheme complies with the requirements of the Voting Rights Act.

The court failed to consider alternative electoral schemes, and an independent review of the various local government electoral systems will establish that at least one method, the single transferable vote system of proportional representation (PR), provides fair representation for all minority groups without encouraging racial segregation or requiring harmful gerrymandering similar to that approved in the court's *Hasidic Jews* decision. Furthermore, an analysis of the relevant federal law demonstrates PR is a legally permissible electoral system in local governments subject to the Voting Rights Act.

FEDERAL LEGAL VOTING STANDARDS OF NONDISCRIMINATION

The Voting Rights Division of the U.S. Department of Justice subsequently recognized two alternative voting systems meet the requirements of the act, and imposed them on several southern local governments to remedy violations of the Voting Rights Act. Cumulative voting provides each elector with a number of votes equal to the total number of seats available, and the elector may apportion his votes among candidates in any manner he or she chooses. Thus, if nine seats are available, the voter may give all nine votes to one candidate, vote once for each of nine different candidates, cast six votes for one candidate and three for another, or assign nine votes in any other combination.[39] The system's purpose is to provide representation for minority groups. In common with PR, the minimum number of votes required to elect a candidate is determined by formula: $Q = (Y/N+1) + 1$, in which Q is the required vote quota, Y is the total number of votes cast, and N is the number of seats available.

A candidate, to be assured of winning an election in a city with a nine-member council, needs one more than 10 percent of the total votes cast, the same proportion of votes required under a PR electoral plan. By calculating its voting strength, nominating the correct number of candidates, and successfully instructing its members to apportion their votes among the office seekers, a cohesive group could attain proportional representation on the city's council. Moreover, as an at-large election system, cumulative voting, in common with PR, potentially provides proportional representation for all minority groups.

This system can produce proportional representation only when each group successfully accomplishes a number of complicated tasks. A group miscalculating its voting strength may nominate either too many or too few candidates. If too many candidates are nominated, the group's members may divide their votes in a manner preventing two or more of the nominees from receiving a sufficient number of voters to ensure their election. Vote splitting may enable another group to elect one of its candidates who otherwise would have been defeated. The same result will occur if a group nominates an insufficient number of candidates.

If each group correctly calculates its voting strength and nominates an appropriate number of candidates, the resulting election reveals the foremost political weakness of the system. In their attempts to avoid the potentially dilutive effects resulting from the nomination of too many candidates, each group will limit its nominations according to its proportional voting strength. In consequence, the groups capable of electing representatives will nominate candidates equivalent to the number of available seats. This practice deprives voters of any significant choice in the election and eliminates the need for the candidates to discuss issues.

LIMITED NOMINATION AND VOTING

The failure of the single-member district system in the nineteenth century to provide proper two-party representation led to the development and use of limited voting. Under this system, each voter must vote for fewer candidates than there are seats on the city council in a primary election and in a general election; the plurality rule determines the winners. As a general rule, limited voting makes it impossible for the largest group or party to win a disproportionate share of the council's seats and enables the largest minority or party to elect one or more candidates. Voters are not allowed to express preferences, and since each voter gives the same support to the candidate least favored as to the candidate most favored, the voter may contribute to the defeat of his or her favorite candidate. In consequence, this system encourages bullet voting—voting for only one candidate.

This system may be used in an at-large election or in districts where two or more members are to be elected. The 1963 New York City charter authorized use of the system to elect two council members in each of the city's five boroughs.[40] No party was allowed to nominate more than one candidate for the two council member at-large positions in each of the city's five boroughs, and an elector could not vote for more than one candidate for a council at-large seat. The Democratic Party and the Republican Party usually each elected one council member at-large in each borough, but three liberal party members in the 1969 election, running on the same ticket with Mayor John V. Lindsay, were elected at the expense of Republican candidates. The U.S. Supreme Court's "one-person, one vote" dictum led to the demise of the voting system because the population of each borough differed.[41]

Limited voting is a crude method for securing minority representation. The system neither guarantees each group or each party will be represented fully in proportion to its voting strength nor prevents a minority from electing a majority of the council members when several strong slates of candidates divide the votes cast. In addition, the system normally provides no representation for independent associations or minority parties other than the largest one. Limited voting in a partisan election may influence the election of a minority council member by throwing some votes to a favored minority party candidate, thereby encouraging all minority party candidates to curry the favor of the majority party.

STV-PR

The single-transferable vote form of proportional representation (STV) was developed by Thomas Hare in London in 1857, and is designed to ensure that any group or party with a common political interest attracting a sizable number of votes will be represented in a legislative body in proportion to its voting strength with mathematical exactness. A voter places a "1" on the ballot opposite the candidate he or she favors the most. The voter places a "2" opposite his or her second choice, and similarly selects according to his or her preferences among the remaining candidates. The voter may cast a vote for all or only some of the candidates seeking office. The voter's ballot generally will count toward the election of his or her highest preference who has not been elected or defeated already.

To be elected, a candidate must receive a number of votes equal to the quota, which is determined by dividing the total number of valid ballots by the number of council members to be elected plus one, plus one. If 100,000 valid ballots are cast to elect a nine-member city council, the quota would be equal to 100,000 divided by 9 + 1+ with 1 added to the result, or 10,001. This formula always produces the smallest number of votes that will ensure a candidate's election no matter how the votes may be distributed among the candidates.

Subsequent to the determination of the quota, ballots are sorted by first choices. If any candidate receives a total of number "1" ballots equal to or exceeding the quota, he or she is declared elected. If a candidate receives more than the quota, the surplus ballots are divided among the remaining candidates according to the second choices indicated. The next step is to declare defeated the candidate with the fewest number "1," votes and any surplus votes are transferred from elected candidates to the remaining candidates according to the next choices marked on them. If a second choice has been elected or defeated, the ballots are distributed to the third choices. A new count is conducted, and any candidate who has a total of number "1" votes and transferred ballots equal to or exceeding the quota is declared elected. His or her surplus, if any, is distributed to the remaining candidates. This process continues until the full council is elected.

Candidates usually are not allowed to exceed the quota during a transfer. Upon reaching the quota, any surplus ballots are given immediately to the next choice before the tabulation of new vote totals. Most ballots, either on the first choice or by transfer, help to elect a candidate. Alternatively, surplus number "1" votes may be distributed according to a formula. The ballots of a candidate with a surplus of number "1" votes are reexamined to determine the distribution of number "2" votes," and the surplus is distributed proportionally according to second choices.

The principal advantage of this electoral system is that it ensures majority rule while guaranteeing minority representation. Other advantages include elimination of gerrymandering as STV is an at-large system with the possible exception of large cities where multimember districts are utilized, facilitation of the election of independent candidates in non-partisan elections who otherwise might not seek election, and reduction of fraud in ballot counting as all ballots are countered centrally by expert tellers under close supervision, and discouragement of bullet voting.

The single-member district system typically results in overrepresentation of the largest political party or group. PR eliminates the need for a primary election in which voter turnout is low, prevents overrepresentation of a political party or group, and obviates the necessity for a municipality to emphasize racial criteria in its attempt to formulate a voting system providing minorities with proportional representation. The other advantages of using PR on a citywide basis are the elimination of the need to redistrict; racial gerrymandering for either benign or discriminatory purposes; and does not encourage segregation, an effect of single-member districts. PR determines a minority group's voting strength by its size, not by its degree of concentration within a section of a city. The system automatically and continuously provides reapportionment, permitting interest group to attain representation in exact proportion to their voting strengths in each election, increasing the probability candidates will be elected on the basis of merit by requiring each voter to rank each candidate in his or her order of preference, thereby eliminating the potential for "bandwagon" voting; a popular candidate cannot carry into office weak or unqualified candidates who are members of the same political party.

CONCLUSIONS

The Voting Rights Section of the U.S. Department of Justice generally continues to seek to have the single-member district system replace an election system found to violate the Voting Rights Act. Clearly, there are alternative electoral systems acceptable under the act. At least one of these alternatives, STV/PR, provides all minority groups, and not just racial ones, with representation in proportion with their numerical voting strengths and avoids the debilitating characteristics of the single-member district system. Although the Department's authority under the act merely enables it either to approve or to reject proposed electoral changes made by state and local governments, it often confers informally with these jurisdictions in the development of their remedial proposals. The department provides indications during these conferences of the type of system it would approve. Unfortunately, as suggested by the 65 percent nonwhite figure promoted by the department's officers in the *Hasidic Jews* case, this advice often is unimaginative and, as observed by U.S. Chief Justice Warren Burger, is unnecessarily rigid in relation to the state's obligation under the act.

There are indications the U.S. Supreme Court may declare unconstitutional the Voting Rights Act as several justices have expressed reservations concerning the act. Chief Justice John Roberts of the U.S. Supreme Court in *Northwest Austin Municipal Utility District No. One v. Holder* in 2009 opined: "the Act also differentiates between the States, despite our historic tradition that all the States enjoy 'equal sovereignty.'"[42] Nevertheless, the Court upheld the constitutionality of the Section 5 preclearance requirement, and reversed the decision of the U.S. District Court for the District of Columbia, holding the utility district was not eligible under the act to bail out of the preclearance requirement.[43] Justice Clarence Thomas wrote he would hold that Section 5 "exceeds Congress' power to enforce the Fifteenth Amendment."[44]

ATLANTIC STRIPED BASE CONSERVATION ACT AMENDMENTS OF 1986

Congress in 1942 granted its consent to the Atlantic States Marine Fisheries Compact uniting fifteen coastal states in a cooperative effort to preserve and improve ocean fisheries.[45] The compact initially was subject to a fifteen-year sunset clause, but Congress removed the clause in 1950. Each member state appoints three commissioners to serve on the compact-created Commission that lacks regulatory powers. The Commission plans to rebuild all fisheries stocks by 2015. Stocks rebuilt by 2011 are Atlantic herring, Atlantic striped bass, black sea bass, bluefish, northern shrimp, and scup.[46]

Congress enacted the Atlantic Striped Bass Conservation Act Amendments of 1986, and added a contingent preemption section, thereby indirectly granting regulatory powers to the Commission.[47] Failure of a state to comply with a commission developed plan automatically results in the U.S. Fish and Wildlife Service and the Marine Fisheries Service imposing a striped bass fishing moratorium in the coastal waters of the noncomplying state(s). This section has been an outstanding success and striped bass have recovered their numbers to their historic high level.[48]

Congress in 1993 concluded the current regulatory scheme "failed to provide adequate protection for other fish species because . . . no single governmental entity has exclusive management authority for Atlantic coastal fisheries resources, harvesting of such resources is frequently subject to disparate, inconsistent, and intermittent State and Federal regulation that has been detrimental to the conservation and sustainable use of such resources and to the interest of fishermen and the Nation as a whole."[49]

Based upon this finding, Congress enacted the Atlantic Coastal Fisheries Cooperative Fisheries Management Act of 1993 containing a second contingent provision directing the Commission to draft fisheries management plans for all migratory fish along the Atlantic coast, and requiring the all coastal states to comply with the plans.[50] The Commission monitors state compliance with its fisheries management plans and reports noncomplying states to the Secretary of Commerce who is authorized impose a moratorium on fishing in the coastal waters of the state for fish species whose plans are not observed by the state. This contingent preemption clause, in common with the 1986 similar clause for striped bass, has been completely successful in encouraging state compliance with the Commission's plans.

The Commission's 2010 annual report reveals considerable success in rebuilding the stocks of scup, summer founder, bluefish, Atlantic croaker, and spiny dogfish.[51] Less success was achieved in rebuilding the stocks of winter flounder, weakfish, tautog, American shad, river herring, and southern New England American lobster.

GRAMM-LEACH-BLILEY FINANCIAL MODERNIZATION ACT OF 1999

The business of insurance in the United States was regulated exclusively by states until 1944, when the U.S. Supreme Court opined the business involves interstate commerce and hence is subject to congressional regulation.[52] States reacted with alarm and lobbied Congress to reverse the Court's decision. The National Association of Insurance Commissioners (NAIC) drafted a proposed law reversing the court's decision and generally restoring the regulatory environment existing prior to the court's decision. Congress in March 1945 enacted the McCarran-Ferguson Act, essentially NAIC's bill, devolving authority to the states to regulate the business of insurance, and exempting states from the Sherman Antitrust Act of 1890, and the Federal Trade Commission Act of 1914 by suspending the operation of the dormant interstate commerce clause.[53]

The continuing lack of uniform state insurance statutes and administrative regulations promoted pressures by the insurance industry on Congress to provide relief in the form of establishment of uniform standards. Although Congress enacted the Gramm-Leach-Bliley Financial Modernization Act of 1999, comprehensively regulating the financial services industry, the act devoted only two sections to insurance.[54] The first section was a contingent preemption one, threatening establishment of federal insurance agent licensing if twenty-six states fail to adopt by November 12, 2002, a uniform licensing system for agents.[55] Thirty states had been certified by September 10, 2002 as having a uniform system, thereby avoiding preemption. The second section established a maximum cap, instead of minimum standards, on the stringency of state insurance regulations in thirteen specified areas.[56]

ENERGY POLICY ACT OF 2008

Electrical energy is in short supply, especially during the summer, in a number of sections of the United States, and is attributable in part to the difficulties encountered by transmission companies in obtaining permits for construction of new electric transmission facilities. Congress responded to this problem by enacting the Energy Policy Act of 2005, with a section devoted to solving the problem.[57]

The act directs the Secretary of Energy to consult with the states, and every three years study electric transmission congestion, and designate geographic areas experiencing constraints on electric energy affecting adversely interstate electric transmission. Failure of a state regulating commission to approve an application for a permit after one year allows the Federal Energy Regulatory Commission to issue a permit.[58] The same section also grants the consent of Congress to three or more contiguous states to enact an interstate electric energy facilities compact, establishing regional transmission siting agencies to facilitate siting and carrying of electricity.[59] The commission has not yet needed to issue a construction permit.[60]

SUMMARY AND CONCLUSIONS

Contingent preemption statutes have been effective in achieving their objectives. The Voting Rights Act of 1965, the first such statute, produced a revolution in terms of the number of black citizens of voting age who registered, voted in elections, and been elected to public office. The Voting Rights Division of the U.S. Department of Justice can be faulted for promoting the single-member district system as a remedy for past wrongs denying black citizens the right to register and to vote when there is an alternative electoral system, the single-transferable vote system of proportional representations, which avoids all of the problems associated with the single-member district systems and provides better representation for the protected classes of citizens and all other voters.

The congressional decision to employ a contingent threat of a fishing moratorium achieved its goal of persuading all Atlantic Coast states to abide by the fisheries plans drafted by the Atlantic States Marine Fisheries Commission. Similarly, the contingent provision in the Gramm-Leach-Bliley Financial Modernization Act quickly persuaded thirty-five states to harmonize their respect systems of licensing insurance agents.

The Federal Energy Regulatory Commission has not employed its authority under the Energy Policy Act of 2005 to issue a permit for the siting of electric energy transmission towers in the event of a state's failure to grant a construction permit within one year of the filing of a construction application. The potential threat of a federal construction permit no doubt encourages states to make accommodations and issue such permits.

Chapter 7 evaluates the effectiveness of innovative preemption statutes, and advocates use of interstate compacts and federal-state compacts to solve many public problems.

Chapter 7

Innovative Congressional Preemption Statutes

An Evaluation

Alexander Hamilton in the Federalist No. 17 maintained on December 5, 1787, "it will always be far more easy for the State governments to encroach upon the national authorities than for the national government to encroach upon the state authorities."[1] Experience has proven the inaccuracy of Hamilton's prediction, as Congress by 2015 enacted 704 preemption statutes removing completely or partially specified regulatory powers from state governments, thereby shifting a considerable amount of decision-making authority from state and local governments to Congress, and increasing national regulatory uniformity. Nevertheless, state legislatures today are regulating matters that did not exist in 1789.

M. J. C. Vile, an English observer, wrote in 1961, "the day-to-day relations between Federal and state governments became the object of congressional attention not as a legislature intent upon curbing state power, but as a legislative body composed of local politicians concerned to defend state power unless a great national problem converts Congress temporarily into a legislature of national statesmen."[2] This statement was generally accurate when written, but is invalid today. The current U.S. federal system is a product of metamorphic federalism, and is still recognizable as an *imperium in imperio* with political powers divided between the national government and the state governments, despite the great accretion of political power by the U.S. government.

Jane Perry Clark wrote an excellent 1936 law review article titled "Interdependent Federal and State Law as a Form of Federal-State

Cooperation," which focused on the "action by which the law of one government is made to depend on that of the other."[3] Subsequently, Congress increasingly became more dependent upon the assistance of state governments to achieve national goals set forth in congressional innovative preemption statutes. The U.S. Constitution contains general wording and does not establish precise and permanent jurisdictional boundary lines delineating the respective powers of the two planes of government. Congressional enactment of preemption statutes, especially post-1965 innovative ones, removed completely or partially specified regulatory powers from state and local governments in the latter decades of the twentieth century and the first decade of the twenty-first century. Seven of the preemption statutes economically deregulated completely the following industries: railroads, airlines, natural gas, motor carriers, buses, telecommunications, and aspects of depository institutions. In other words, these industries are not subject to economic regulation by Congress and by state legislatures. Furthermore, congressional devolution of powers to states produced major changes in nature of the federal system without the use of constitutional amendments, with three exceptions. The framers of the U.S. Constitution purposely did not include in the fundamental law a mechanism for ensuring a continuing balance between the powers of Congress and the powers of the states as they recognized the undesirability of a static distribution of political powers. They also were aware there would be controversies between two or more states on occasions, and therefore granted the U.S. Supreme Court original (trial) jurisdiction over such controversies.

The U.S. Supreme Court has employed the Fourteenth Amendment since the mid-1920s to incorporate most of the constitutional Bill of Rights into the Amendment in order to protect the rights of citizens against abridgment by subnational governments. The Fifteenth Amendment guarantees the voting rights of black citizens, and the Seventeenth Amendment provides for the popular election of all U.S. senators. The current complex and metamorphic ongoing changes in the federal system would baffle the framers of the U.S. Constitution, yet the system reveals the framers designed a flexible Constitution allowing Congress to respond to changing national conditions and world conditions.

Congress initially assisted state governments to solve a wide variety of problems, including environmental ones, by means of conditional grants-in-aid, tax credits for initiating a specified action, and cross-over sanctions reducing a specific federal grants-in-aid to a state for failure to take a congressionally identified action in another specified regulatory field. The continuing failure of state governments to solve a number of major problems transcending state boundary lines increased political pressure on Congress to enact statutes designed to directly or to indirectly solve each of these problems. The resulting expansion of the powers of Congress is revealed clearly in the declared purposes of the Americans with Disabilities Act of 1990:

1. to provide a clear and comprehensive national mandate for the elimination of discrimination against individuals with disabilities;

2. to provide clear, strong, consistent, enforceable standards addressing discrimination against individuals with disabilities;

3. to ensure that the Federal Government plays a central role in enforcing the standards established in this Act on behalf of individuals with disabilities; and

4. to invoke the sweep of congressional authority, including the power to enforce the fourteenth amendment and to regulate commerce, in order to address the major areas of discrimination faced day-to-day by people with disabilities.[4]

A number of congressional complete preemption statutes contain a savings clause exempting one or more specified matters from preemption. States legislatures today have less authority with respect to their original unrestrained freedom to exercise all regulatory powers reserved to them by the U.S. Constitution in 1789. Nevertheless, individual state legislatures continue to enact statutes based upon their reserved powers that have not been completely preempted and to enact statutes in areas partially preempted, thereby continuing to serve as laboratories of democracies generating innovative solutions for public problems that often are adopted by sister-state legislatures and Congress. As noted, state governments and local governments provide all public services to citizens, with the exception of the postal service, which is the only service directly provided to citizens by the U.S. Government within states.

Centripetal and centrifugal forces combine to produce constantly changing patterns of relations between the national government and the state governments, and between the state governments and their respective local governments. The federal system nevertheless retains elements of a unitary system and elements of a confederate system as intended by the drafters of the U.S. Constitution. Intergovernmental cooperation continues to be essential for the health of the federal system.

Increasing centralization of political power in the national government in the period 1935 to 1970 is attributable primarily to congressional enactment of statutes containing conditional grants-in-aid and conditional tax credits for subnational governments. Although Congress has enacted preemption acts since 1790, they generally had relatively little impact on the federal system prior to congressional enactment of minimum standards preemption statutes commencing in 1965, and other types of preemption statutes: complete, contingent, economic deregulation of specific industries, maximum standards, and more stringent state standards without agency advanced approval. The minimum standards preemption approach is based on the "gun behind the door" theory of limited preemption. The approach also can be labeled contingent complete preemption, as the failure of a state to enforce the national minimum standards or enforce higher state standards results in the state's loss of all regulatory authority in the field.

Daniel J. Elazar in 1984 identified three political cultures in the United States—individualistic, moralistic, and traditionalist—and classified each state by its political culture, thereby helping to explain individual state acceptance of or resistance to congressional preemption statutes, particularly ones containing mandates and restraints.[5] In 1992, he wrote to the author and commented, "[y]our addition of federal mandates and preemption to the older theories of dual and cooperative federalism is quite helpful."[6]

Congress continues to play three roles—inhibitor, initiator, and facilitator—when interacting with states, and the U.S. federal system continues to evolve from its original form when there were limited symbiotic contacts between the two planes of government to a system containing additional characteristics of a unitary system. Nevertheless, the federal system retains many of its original features, including interdependence of the two planes of government. Minimum standards preemption in particular has had a major impact on the nature of the governance system by reinvigorating it, particularly by the development of innovative types of such preemption commencing in 1965.

Citizens generally experience few difficulties in understanding the nature of a unitary governance system. The initial federal system was considerably more complex than a unitary system, and the complexity was increased greatly by the enactment of innovative preemption statutes commencing in 1965. The current systemic complexity of the federal system with overlapping federal authority and state authority, and its kaleidoscopic nature baffle most citizens. Dissatisfied citizens often are unable to determine the government responsible for the failure to achieve statutory goals. In consequence, the ability of voters to control congressional regulatory policy-making has become more difficult with the enactment of such statutes. There is little evidence, however, that governmental accountability and responsibility in regulatory fields are lacking.

Many public problems solved by congressional enactment of preemption statutes could have been solved alternatively by means of enactment of interstate compacts and/or federal-state interstate compacts.

INTERSTATE COMPACTS

The drafters of the U.S. Constitution recognized the importance of interstate cooperation in the proposed federal system, and included in the fundamental law authorization for two or more states to enter into interstate agreements or compacts with the consent of Congress.[7] The reader should note an interstate compact can be utilized to achieve the same goal(s) as a regulatory preemption statute, provided all state legislatures enact the concerned regulatory compact. An interstate compact also can be employed in some instances to achieve the same goal as a U.S. constitutional amendment, as illustrated by the proposed Interstate Agreement to Elect the President by National Popular Vote.[8]

Formal and informal interstate cooperation and formal and informal federal-state cooperation are common, and together often solve major public problems, as well as minor public problems. The reader should be aware there are also exceptionally large numbers of informal interstate agreements and informal federal-state agreements, including written and verbal cooperative efforts to control and/or to eliminate organized crime, designed to provide mutual assistance, and to prevent environmental pollution among other objectives. Such cooperation should not blind the reader to the fact that interstate disputes and federal-state disputes are relatively common.

Felix Frankfurter and James Landis in 1925 noted "the combined legislative powers of Congress and of the several states permit a wide range of permutations and combinations for governmental action. Until very recently these potentialities have been left largely unexplored. . . . Creativeness is called for to devise a great variety of legal alternatives to cope with the diverse forms of interstate interests."[9] Their suggestion first was adopted in 1962, when the Delaware River Basin Compact, the first federal-interstate state compact linking the U.S. government and four state governments, was enacted by Congress and the state legislature in Delaware, New Jersey, New York, and Pennsylvania, thereby mobilizing the resources of all compact members to address a major public problem.[10]

Alternatives to the use of an interstate compact or a federal-state compact to solve a problem(s) include all state legislatures enacting parallel statutes, or uniform statutes, or reciprocity statutes, and interstate administrative agreements.[11] Unfortunately, the number of such statutes enacted by all fifty state legislatures is relatively small, and Congress decided to provide more uniformity of governmental regulatory policies in selected regulatory fields by means of preemption statutes.

INNOVATIVE CONGRESSIONAL PREEMPTION STATUTES

Congress by enactment of preemption statutes removing regulatory powers from state governments has become the supreme regulator with respect to interstate commerce with a very high percentage of the statutes designed to improve the flow of interstate commerce. The first two preemption acts, copyrights and patents, removed all regulatory powers in these two fields from the states. Congress also enacted partial preemption statutes removing from states their regulatory powers in part of each preempted field. This volume focuses on innovative partial preemption acts, first enacted in 1965, establishing a new type of national-state regulatory partnership.

Each congressional preemption act, except economic deregulating ones, typically is an outline law establishing a national policy in a regulatory field in broad terms. The secretary of the concerned U.S. department or the administrator of the concerned U.S. agency is granted authority by Congress to promulgate detailed implementing rules and regulations, thereby enhancing their respective regulatory roles.

Congress on occasion enacts a preemption statute de novo without considering the effectiveness of similar types of previously enacted preemption statutes or their potential unforeseen adverse regulatory effects on state governments and local governments. For example, the Airline Deregulation Act of 1978 was interpreted by the U.S. Supreme Court as a field preemption statute depriving state attorneys general of authority individually and collectively to enforce state deceptive practices laws against airlines that was effective.[12] In 2001 and 2002, the importance of state regulation was demonstrated by the New York attorney general, who revealed the ineffectiveness of the U.S. Security and Exchange Commission, empowered by nine congressional statutes, to police the banking industry adequately.[13]

INNOVATIVE MINIMUM STANDARDS PARTIAL PREEMPTION ACTS

This volume explains and evaluates congressional statutes partially preempting the regulatory authority of states relative to water quality, drinking-water quality, air quality, surface mining and reclamation of mined lands, maximum state regulatory authority standards, congressional regulatory authority turn-backs to states, and state-friendly preemption statutes. The evidence presented supports the general conclusion that congressional complete, partial, minimum standards, and contingent preemption acts improved the quality of governmental regulation in each preempted field. The minimum standards approach encourages state legislatures to exercise what had been latent powers simultaneously with the loss of their freedom to exercise other specific regulatory powers as the result of preemption. Unfortunately, problems still remain in each of the innovative minimum standards preemption fields. Debates also continue relative to the proper roles of Congress and state legislatures in engaging in regulatory activities to solve major public problems extending across state boundary lines.

WATER QUALITY

The substantial improvement in general water quality is attributable to the new innovative type of national-state partnership established in 1965. The congressional minimum standards partial preemption approach was revolutionary at that time. The required permit for discharging water, in particular, has proven to be effective in reducing the flow of pollutants into waterways, but does not apply to returns of water from irrigated agricultural lands, a reflection of the political power of farmers in Congress. Recognizing enforcement of the Water Quality Act of 1965 by the national government and state governments may be ineffective, Congress granted standing to citizens to sue polluters in the U.S. District Court for violating a provision(s) of the act.

The large geographically diverse area of the United States (3,628,159 square miles) and the wide variety of weather conditions in sections of the nation make the establishment of uniform water pollution abatement programs difficult. Studies, including ones by the U.S. Government Accountability Office, not surprisingly, reveal the U.S. Environmental Protection Agency's regional offices were inconsistent in enforcing the Clean Water Act. The Agency acknowledges the difficulty of determining whether water quality is improving.

The congressional Drinking Water Act seeks to improve the quality of drinking water throughout the nation, but has been plagued by problems similar to those of the general water-quality program, including inaccurate reporting of violations. Approximately forty-five million people are drinking water from small drinking water systems that Congress exempted from the act. Furthermore, numerous drinking water systems are old and are responsible for poor-quality drinking water.

The Surface Mining and Reclamation Act of 1977 has restored to a large extent the damage caused by surface mining and has reduced the runoff of water from mining areas. Nevertheless, a major problem—acid mining drainage into waters—has not been solved.

The U.S. Advisory Commission on Intergovernmental Relations in 1984 published a report examining the growth of intergovernmental regulations, its legal foundation, its legislative origins, its implementation, and its impact of national intergovernmental regulation. The commission advanced recommendations to reform the intergovernmental regulation system and make it more effective in terms of goal achievement.[14] Enforcement was identified by the commission as "the weakest link" in intergovernmental regulations. The Commission concluded:

> As a general rule, . . . federal intergovernmental regulations have proven difficult to enforce, statutory deadlines have been repeatedly extended or ignored, and compliance—though probably better than one would anticipate, given the generally haphazard character of federal supervision—has fallen short of official expectations. Such shortcomings in performance account for the Doctor Jekyll and Mr. Hyde reputation of the Office of Civil Rights (OCR) and many other federal regulatory agencies. OCR has been regarded as a hotbed of regulatory zealots by one set of critics and as a timed, lumbering bureaucracy by another. Both are correct—but each is looking at a different aspect of the process.[15]

The Commission attributed the enforcement problems to "administrative and technical problems, a lack of adequate resources, and political obstacles to the imposition of sanctions."[16] The report is thirty years old, yet it remains generally accurate, and probably will be accurate for the foreseeable future. The U.S. government's bureaucratic regulatory behemoth has major administrative and technical problems. Furthermore, Congress never has provided administrative departments and agencies with adequate resources to execute in a most efficient and effective manner their numerous assigned responsibilities, particularly supervision of the compliance of states granted regulatory primacy with the different minimum standards established by Congress and implementing rules and regulations promulgated for each regulatory program.

The reader should keep in mind that Congress is a political body influenced by interest groups. Great pressure is brought to bear on Congress to grant extensions of time to achieve statutory goals or to grant complete or partial exemption from regulatory standards for specified activities, including run off of water from agricultural lands and emissions of sulfur dioxide from coal-burning electrical generating plants that produce acid rain and result in the death of marine life in mountain lakes and ponds.

AIR QUALITY

Congress in the Air Quality Act of 1967 incorporated the same type of minimum standards preemption provisions as are contained in the Water Quality Act of 1965. The motor vehicle manufacturers were fearful each state legislature would enact nonuniform air-quality statutes requiring motor vehicle emissions to meet differing standards. In consequence, they lobbied Congress to preempt completely the authority of each state to establish emission standards.

The 1967 act mandated the achievement of specified reductions in the emissions of air pollutants without considering the economic feasibility and the technical feasibility of the standards. The act also forbade each state to allow the release of emissions that would contribute to a sister state's failure to meet the national minimum air-quality standards.

Congress amended the act in 1977 and in 1990. The evidence reveals the minimum standards preemption approach significantly reduced air pollution. One of the most successful air pollution reduction actions was the 1990 congressional authorization for the trading of air emission pollution allowances effective in 1995. This initiative stands in sharp contrast to the prior command-and-control approach requiring pollution sources to install emission control equipment, or to construct replacement facilities emitting fewer pollutants into the air. The initiative's purpose is to encourage electric generating companies to construct coal-fired power plants emitting less sulfur dioxide or to install new pollution abatement equipment at existing plants. A company, by lowering emissions of sulfur dioxide below the maximum allowable by the act and promulgated regulations, gains allowances salable to companies owning plants emitting more than the allowable amount of this pollutant, pending construction of new plants emitting less pollution. This approach encourages the owners of older facilities emitting air pollutants to replace the facilities with new, more effective facilities.

CRITICISMS OF CONGRESS AND THE EXECUTIVE BRANCH.

It is not surprising that state and local government officers, including elected officers, have been critical of the leadership role of Congress and the executive branch in their attempts to solve environmental problems. Robert L. Glickman has been particularly critical of the federal government role, and in 2006 wrote:

> Congress and the Executive Branch . . . have contributed to the decline in federal authority to protect the environment. The assault on federal power has come from many directions. Congress has narrowed the responsibilities of some federal agencies to consider the adverse environmental implications of their decisions by creating categorical exclusions from NEPA [National Environmental Policy Act of 1969]. It also has exempted some federal activities, primarily military activities, from pre-existing statutory constraints on their ability to pollute. In addition, Congress has made it more difficult for federal agencies, such as EPA, to restrict environmentally damaging conduct by others, in part by burying those agencies under a mountain of analytical paperwork and requiring agencies to employ analytical techniques that are inherently inimical to the protection of environmental values that are difficult to quantify. The Bush Administration has pursued a series of initiatives, in both the pollution and federal lands contexts, that make it more difficult for the federal government to prevent environmental harm, including adoption of weaker regulations, the reduction of funds for environmental protection purposes, and a failure to enforce environmental laws and regulations against alleged violators.[17]

CONCLUDING COMMENTS

The evidence presented in this volume highlights the great flexibility of the U.S. Constitution in allowing restructuring of parts of the federal system without the need for constitutional amendments, in order to solve newly emerging governmental problems. The highlighted innovative partial preemption statutes authorize multijurisdictional governmental bodies to solve various environmental problems. If it so desired, Congress could exercise complete hegemony in solving these problems, but wisely decided to enter into a regulatory partnership with the states that allows each one to tailor its environmental regulatory program, to an extent, to cope with specific or unique problems. In effect, Congress employs the leadership feedback theory by enacting an environmental preemption statute and subsequently possibly amending the statute based upon feedback from state governments, local governments, interest groups, and citizens.

The objective of a minimum standards preemption statute is to form an administrative regulatory partnership between the national government and each state that releases their respective synergies. To date, most states have applied for and received regulatory primacy under the various minimum standards preemption acts. Collectively, these statutes have produced revolutionary changes in national-state relations and comport with the theory of cooperative federalism that needs to be expanded by a broader theory. Minimum standards preemption and delegation of regulatory primacy are compromises between the Scylla of complete centralization of regulatory powers in Congress and the Charybdis of complete decentralization of political power. This preemption type relieves states of responsibility for solving a difficult problem, if they so choose, and also affords a state the opportunity to register a complaint with the concerned national agency that another state is not in compliance with a congressional preemption statute and/or implementing rules and regulations.

Critics of minimum standards preemption statutes contend the concerned statutes and voluminous implementing administrative rules and regulations unnecessarily reduce states' discretionary regulatory authority, contain inadequate provisions for subnational governmental input into the enactment of the congressional statutes and the promulgation of implementing rules and regulations, result in general federal bureaucratic dominance, burden states and local governments with inflexible programmatic requirements, and raise the question of which government is accountable to citizens for failures to achieve environmental goals. Nevertheless, a balanced assessment of innovative minimum standards preemption acts leads to the conclusions such acts have been more successful in achieving their respected listed goals than the earlier command and control regulatory acts, and the excise of political power by state legislatures has increased. The large number of congressional preemption statutes, surprisingly, has resulted in direct U.S. government administration of only a few programs today that it was not responsible for administering prior to 1965.

In sum, innovative national minimum preemption environmental standards have increased environmental regulatory uniformity in the nation while allowing a degree of diversity in state regulatory standards to address particular problems in each state. We conclude the federal system has proven to be a resilient system in addressing effectively new environmental challenges. However, it is important to note that democratic theory is premised on citizens playing an active and an informed role in the governance system. The current Daedalian complexity and fluidity of relations between the national government and state governments, particularly the asymmetrical relations between the former government and individual states, baffles many citizens and reduces their ability to perform an informed governance role.

Notes

CHAPTER 1

1. Joseph F. Zimmerman, *Congressional Preemption: Regulatory Federalism* (Albany: State University of New York Press, 2005).

2. Copyright Act of 1790, 1 Stat. 124, 17 U.S.C. §101, Patent Act of 1790, 1 Stat. 109, 35 U.S.C. 1, and Atomic Energy Act of 1946, 60 Stat. 755, 42 U.S.C.§2011.

3. For a typology of complete congressional preemption statutes, consult Zimmerman, *Congressional Preemption: Regulatory Federalism*: 73–87.

4. Voting Rights Act of 1965, 79 Stat. 437, 42 U.S.C.§1973.

5. Consult Joseph F. Zimmerman, *Contemporary American Federalism: The Growth of National Power*, 2nd ed. (Albany: State University of New York Press, 2008).

6. Consult the writings of James Madison in *The Federalist Papers* (New York: New American Library, 1961).

7. Thomas A. Bailey, *The American Pageant: A History of the Republic*, 3rd ed. (Boston: D. C. Heath, 1967): 136.

8. Ibid., 137.

9. *Virginia v. Tennessee*, 148 U.S. 503, 13 S.Ct. 728 (1893).

10. *Michelin Tire Corporation v. Wages*, 423 U.S. 276 at 286, 96 S.Ct. 535 at 541 (1975).

11. *R. J. Reynolds Tobacco Company v. Durham County*, 479 U.S. 130, 107 S.Ct. 499 (1986).

12. *The Federalist Papers* (New York: New American Library, 1961).

13. Ibid., 119.

14. Ibid., 204.

15. Ibid., 246.

16. Ibid., 282–85.

17. Ibid., 292, 296.

18. Ralph Ketcham, ed. *The Antifederalist Papers and the Constitutional Convention Debates* (New York: New American Library, 1986).

19. Ibid., 272.

20. Alan V. Briceland, "Virginia's Ratification of the U.S. Constitution," *Newsletter* 61 (Institute of Government, University of Virginia, October 1984): 2.

21. Gaillard Hunt, ed. *The Writings of James Madison*, vol. vi (New York: G. P. Putnam's Sons, 1901): 333.

22. *McCulloch v. Maryland*, 4 U.S. 316 at 421, 4 Wheaton 316 at 421 (1819).

23. "New Evidence on the Presumption Against Preemption: An Empirical Study of Congressional Responses to Supreme Court Preemption Decisions," *Harvard Law Review* 120 (2007): 1613.

24. *Hines v. Davidowitz*, 312 U.S. 52 at 67, 61 S.Ct. 399 at 405 (1941).

25. Consult Zimmerman, *Congressional Preemption: Regulatory Federalism*. See also Thomas W. Merrill, "Preemption and Institutional Choice," *Northwestern University Law Review* 102, no. 2 (2008): 727–80; and Erin O'Hara O'Connor and Larry E. Ribstein, "Preemption and Choice of Law Coordination," *Michigan Law Review* 111 (March 2013): 647–713.

26. North American Free Trade Implementation Act of 1993, 107 Stat. 2057, 19 U.S.C.§3303.

27. Patricia M. Crotty, "The New Federalism Game: Primary Implementation of Environmental Policy," *Publius: The Journal of Federalism* 17 (Spring 1987): 53–67.

28. Air Quality Act of 1967, 81 Stat. 465, 42 U.S.C.§1857.

29. Commercial Motor Vehicle Act of 1986, 100 Stat. 3207, 49 U.S.C.§2701.

30. Clean Air Act Amendments of 1990, 104 Stat. 2399, 42 U.S.C.§§7407, 7511c.

31. An example is the Internet Tax Freedom Amendments Act of 2007, 121 Stat. 1024, 47 U.S.C.§609.

32. Zimmerman, *Congressional Preemption*, 73–87.

33. Hazardous Materials Transportation Safety and Security Reauthorization Act of 2005, 119 Stat. 1895, 49 U.S.C.§5103a(g)(s).

34. Water Quality Act of 1965, 79 Stat. 903, 33 U.S.C.§1151. For a list of detailed requirements for a state to gain regulatory primacy, see chapter 4, relative to drinking water.

35. Copyright Act of 1790, 1 Stat. 124, and Patent Act of 1790, 1 Stat. 109.

36. Joseph F. Zimmerman, "Congressional Preemption During the George W. Bush Administration," *Publius: The Journal of Federalism* 37 (Summer 2007): 432–52.

37. Unfunded Mandates Reform Act of 1995, 109 Stat. 48, 2 U.S.C.§1501.

38. Safe Drinking Water Act Amendments of 1996, 110 Stat. 1613, 42 U.S.C.§330f.

39. *United States v. Shimer*, 367 U.S. 374 at 381–82, 81 S.Ct. 1554 at 1560 (1961).

40. Nina A Mendelson, "A Presumption Against Agency Preemption," *Northwestern University Law Review* 102 (2008): 722, 725.

41. Consumer Product Safety Improvement Act of 2008, 122 Stat. 3070, 15 U.S.C.§2051.

42. Ocean Dumping Ban Act of 1988, 102 Stat. 4138, 33 U.S.C.§1401A.

43. Unfunded Mandates Act of 1995, 109 Stat. 48, 2 U.S.C.§1501.

44. Safe Drinking Water Act Amendments of 1986, 100 Stat. 651, 42 U.S.C.§300.

45. New York Laws of 1921, chapter. 649, *New York General Business Law*, §352.

46. Joseph F. Zimmerman, *The Silence of Congress: State Taxation of Interstate Commerce* (Albany: State University of New York Press, 2007).

47. David M. Welborn, *Governance of Federal Regulatory Agencies* (Knoxville: University of Tennessee Press, 1977).

48. *Consumer Product Safety Commission: Administrative Structure Could Benefit from Change* (Washington, DC: U.S. General Accounting Office, 1987) [GAO/HRD-87-14].

49. Ibid., 22.

50. Robert S. Adler, "From 'Model Agency' to Basket Case—Can the Consumer Product Safety Commission Be Redeemed?" *Administrative Law Review* 41 (Winter 1989): 91–92.

51. Douglas R. Williams, "Toward Regional Governance in Environmental Law," *Akron Law Review* 46 (2013): 1047–089.

52. Paul L. Ford, ed. *The Writings of Thomas Jefferson*, vol. 9 (New York: G. P. Putnam, 1898): 452.

53. Joseph F. Zimmerman, *Congress: Facilitator of State Action* (Albany: State University of New York Press, 2010).

54. *Commission on Intergovernmental Relations: A Report to the President for Transmittal to the Congress* (Washington, DC: U.S. Government Printing Office, 1955): 63–64.

55. Ibid., 70.

56. Water Quality Act of 1965, 79 Stat. 903, 33 U.S.C.§1151.

57. Atomic Energy Act of 1959, 73 Stat. 688, 42 U.S.C.§2021.

58. Regulatory Federalism: Policy, Powers, Impact, and Reform (Washington, DC: U.S. Advisory Commission on Intergovernmental Relations, 1984): 259.

59. Richard S. Williamson, "The Self-Government Balancing Act: A View from the White House," *National Civic Review* 71 (January 1982): 19.

60. Joseph F. Zimmerman, "Federal Preemption Under Reagan's New Federalism," *Publius: The Journal of Federalism* 21 (Winter 1991): 7–28.

CHAPTER 2

1. Water Quality Act of 1965, 79 Stat. 907, 33 U.S.C.§204.

2. 1 Stat. 138 (1790).

3. 2 Stat. 225 (1803).

4. 2 Stat. 490 (1803).

5. 5 Stat. 201 (1837).

6. 3 Stat. 430 (1818).

7. Morrill Act of 1862, 12 Stat. 503.

8. Hatch Act of 1887, 24 Stat. 440, 7 U.S.C.§362.

9. Carey Act of 1894, 28 Stat. 422, 43 U.S.C.§641.

10. Weeks Act of 1911, 36 Stat. 961, 16 U.S.C.§552.

11. Federal Road Aid Act of 1916, 39 Stat. 355.

12. 42 Stat. 212 (1921).

13. Hayden-Cartwright Act of 1934, 48 Stat. 993.

14. Social Security Act of 1935, 49 Stat. 620, 301.

15. Hatch Act of 1939, 53 Stat. 1147, 5 U.S.C.§118i; and Hatch Act of 1940, 54 Stat. 7767, 5 U.S.C.§118i.

16. Federal Good, Drug, and Cosmetic Act of 1938, 52 Stat. 1020, 21 U.S.C.§301.

17. *Caraker v. Sandoz Pharmaceutical Corporation*, 172 F. Supp.2d 1018 at 1033 (S.D. Ill, 2001).

18. The Act of June 2, 1879, 21 Stat. 7. For details on efforts to control water pollution, consult William L. Andreen, "The Evolution of Water Pollution Control in the United States—State, Local, and Federal Efforts, 1789–1972: Part II," *Stanford Environmental Law Journal* 22 (2003): 215–94.

19. Rivers and Harbors Act of 1886, 24 Stat. 310, and Rivers and Harbors Act of 1899, 30 Stat. 1151. The latter act was referred to popularly as the Refuse Act.

20. Water Quality Act of 1965, 79 Stat. 903, 33 U.S.C.§1151. The act initially made the Secretary of the Interior responsible for administration of the act. Upon the creation of the Environmental Protection Agency, responsibility for administration of the act was transferred to the Agency.

21. Ibid.

22. Jack McCarthy, "Manure Flow Raises Worry," *The Press Enterprise* (Riverside, California) (April 18, 1998): B3.

23. "Randolph Board Sets Stricter Hog Standards," *Greensboro News 7 Record* (North Carolina) (March 24, 1998): B1.

24. Lawrence S. Bazel, "The Clean Water Act at Thirty: A Failure After All These Years," *Natural Resources & Environment* 46 (2003): 46–50.

25. Mark Atlas, "Enforcement Principles and Environmental Agencies: Principal-Agent Relationships in a Delegated Environmental Program," *Law & Society Review* 41, no. 4 (2007): 241.

26. Water Pollution Control Act Amendments of 1972, 70 Stat. 498, 33 U.S.C.§1151.

27. Clean Water Act of 1977, 91 Stat 1577, 33 U.S.C.§13421.

28. Patricia M. Crotty, "The New Federalism Game: Options for the States." Paper presented at the annual meeting of the Northeastern Political Science Association, Philadelphia, November 14–16, 1985.

29. Consult Patrick S. Cawley, "The Diminished Need for Citizen Suits to Enforce the Clean Water Act, *Journal of Legislation* 25 (1999): 181–94.

30. Jennifer L. Seidenberg, "Texas Independent Producers & Royalty Owners Association v. Environmental Protection Agency: Redefining the Role of Public Participation in the Clean Water Act," *Ecology Law Quarterly* 33 (2006): 723.

31. Water Quality Act of 1987, 101 Stat. 76, 33 U.S.C.§1251.

32. Ocean Pollution Reduction Act of 1994, 108 Stat. 4396, 33 U.S.C.§1311. See also Katherine A. Swanson, "The Cost of Doing Business: Corporate Vicarious Criminal Liability for the Negligent Discharge of Oil Under the Clean Water Act," *Washington Law Review* 84 (2009): 555–79.

33. Clean Water Act of 1977, 91 Stat. 1577, 33 U.S.C.§13421.

34. Scott D. Anderson, "Watershed Management and Non Point Source Pollution: The Massachusetts Approach," *Environmental Affairs* 26 (1999): 341–86. See 385, in particular.

35. *Clean Water Act: Longstanding Issues Impact EPA's and States' Enforcement Efforts* (Washington, DC: U.S. Government Accountability Office, 2009) [GAO-10-165T]. See also *Federal Water Requirements: Challenges to Estimating the Cost Impact on Local Communities* (Washington, DC: U.S. Government Accountability Office, 2005) [GAO-06-151R].

36. Katharine Q. Seelye, "U.S. Report Faults Efforts to Trace Water Pollution," *New York Times* (May 27, 2003): 1, A19.

37. Guy Gugliotta and Eric Pianin, "EPA: Few Fined for Polluting Water," *Washington Post* (June 6, 2003): 1.

38. *Assessing and Reporting Water Quality Questions and Answers* (Washington, DC: U.S. Environmental Protection Agency, 2011): 4.

39. Ibid.

40. Robert W. Adler, Resilience, Restoration, and Responsibility: Revisiting the Fundamental Principles of the Clean Water Act," *Washington University Journal of Law and Policy* 32 (2010): 172.

41. *Clean Water Act: Longstanding Issues Impact EPA's and States' Enforcement Efforts* (Washington, DC: U.S. Government Accountability Office, 2009): 4 [GAO-10-1651].

42. Ibid., 12–13.

43. Henry M. Butler and Jonathan Macey, "Externalities and the Matching Principle: The Case for Reallocating Environmental Regulatory Authority," *Yale Law & Policy Review* 14, no. 2 (1996): 59.

44. *Great Lakes Restoration Initiative: Further Actions Would Result in More Useful Assessments and Help Address Factors that Limit Progress* (Washington, DC: U.S. Government Accountability Office 2013).

45. Ibid., 52–53.

46. Ibid., 54–55.

47. American Coal Foundation, *Fast Facts About Coal*, www.teachcoal.org.

48. *West Virginia Laws of 1939*, chap. 84; *Ohio Laws of 1947*, chap. 730, and *Kentucky Laws of 1954*, chap. 8.

49. 121 *Congressional Record* 15, 421 (1975).

50. Surface Mining and Control and Reclamation Act of 1977, 91 Stat. 445, 30 U.S.C.§1201. For the early history of the act, consult Edward M. Green, "State and Federal Roles Under the Surface Mining Control and Reclamation Act of 1977," *Southern Illinois University Law Journal* 21 (1997): 531–51. *Bragg v. West Virginia Coal Association*, 248 F.3d 275 (2001). This decision was upheld by the U.S. Supreme Court in 2002. See *Bragg v. West Virginia Coal Association*, 534 U.S. 112, 122 S.Ct. 920 (2002).

52. *Hodel v. Virginia Surface Mining and Reclamation Association*, 452 U.S. 264 at 288, 101 S.Ct. 2353 at 2366 (1981).

53. *Directives System* (Washington, DC: Office of Surface Mining, U.S. Department of the Interior, 2011).

54. Barbara S. Webber and David J. Webber, "Promoting Economic Incentives for Environmental Protection in the Surface Mining Control and Reclamation Act of 1977: An Analysis of the Design and Implementation of Reclamation of Performance Bonds, *Natural Resources Journal* 25 (April 1985): 389–414.

55. For a case study of the act, consult Theodore M. Vestal, "Federal Administration of the Surface Mining Control and Reclamation Act of 1977 in Oklahoma," *Publius: The Journal of Federalism* 18 (Winter 1988): 45–60.

56. *Directives System*.

57. Ibid., A-2.

58. "Improving EPA Review of Appalachian Surface Coal Mining Operations Under the Clean Water Act, National Environmental Policy Act, and the Environmental Justice Executive Order" (Washington, DC: U.S. Environmental Protection Agency, 2011).

59. Ibid., 4.

60. John C. Dernbach, "Pennsylvania's Implementation of the Surface Mining Control and Reclamation Act: An Assessment of How 'Cooperative Federalism' Can Make State Regulatory Programs More Effective," *University of Michigan Journal of Law Reform* 19 (1986): 965–67.

61. Ibid.

62. Charles E. Davis, Sandra K. Davis, and Denise Peacock, "State Implementation of the Surface Mining and Control and Reclamation Act of 1977," *Policy Studies Review* 9 (Autumn 1989): 110–11.

63. Ibid., 117.

64. Edward M. Green, "State and Federal Roles Under the Surface Mining Control and Reclamation Act of 1977," *Southern Illinois University Law Journal* 21 (1997): 532.

65. James L. Sams III and Kevin M. Beer, *Effects of Coal-Mine Drainage on Stream Water Quality in the Allegheny and Monongahela River Basins—Sulfate Transport and Trends* (Lemoyne, PA: National Water-Quality Assessment Program, 2000).

66. Ibid., 16.

67. Robert W. Adler, "The Lost Books in the Water Quality Trilogy: The Elusive Objectives of Physical and Biological Integrity," *Environmental Law* 33 (2003): 29.

68. *Hardock Mining: BLM Needs to Better Manage Financial Assurances to Guarantee Coverage of Reclamation Costs.* (Washington, DC: U.S. Government Accountability Office, 2005).

69. Ibid., 7.

70. Ibid., 66.

71. *Surface Coal Mining: Financial Assurances for, and Long-Term Oversight of, Mines with Valley Fills in Four Appalachian States* (Washington, DC: U.S. Government Accountability Office, 2010) [GAO-10-206].

72. *Surface Coal Mining: Characteristics of Mining in Mountainous Areas of Kentucky and West Virginia* (Washington, DC: U.S. Government Accountability Office, 2010): 2.

73. Will Reisinger, Trenta A. Dougherty, and Nolan Moser, "Environmental Enforcement and the Limits of Cooperative Federalism: Will Courts Allow Citizens Suits to Pick up the Slack?" *Duke Environmental Law & Policy Forum* 20 (Winter 2010): 24.

74. Ibid., 25.

75. "Testimony of Mr. Mike Carey before the Subcommittee on Water Resources and Environment of the U.S. House of Representatives on EPA Mining Policies: Assault on Appalachian Jobs Part II, May 11, 2011" (Columbus: Ohio Coal Association, 2011).

76. *Drinking Water: Unreliable State Data Limit EPA's Ability to Target Enforcement Priorities and Communicate Water Systems Performance* (Washington, DC: U.S. Government Accountability Office, 2011): 5.

77. Safe Drinking Water Act of 1974, 88 Stat. 1665, 42 U.S.C.§201

78. 40 *Code of Federal Regulations* 142, subpart B.

79. E-mail message from Caryn Muellerteile of the U.S. Environmental Protection Agency, August 8, 2011.

80. Ibid., 88 Stat. 1676, 42 U.S.C.§300h.

81. Brigham Daniels, Erika Weinthal, and Blake Hudson, "Is an Exemption from US Groundwater Regulations a Loophole or a Noose?" *Policy Sci* 41 (2008): 205–20.

82. Ibid., 217.

83. Safe Drinking Water Act of 1974, 88 Stat. 1665, 42 U.S.C.§300h. For details, consult Markus G. Puder and Michel J. Paque, "Tremors in the Cooperative Environmental Federalism Arena: What Happens When a State Wants to Assume Only Portions of a Primacy Program or Return a Primacy Program?—The Underground Injection Control Program under the Safe Drinking Water Act as a Case Study." *Temple Journal of Science, Technology & Environmental Law* 24 (2005): 71–92.

84. Safe Drinking Water Act Amendments of 1986, 100 Stat. 651, 42 U.S.C.§300g.

85. Ibid., 110 Stat. 1613, 42 U.S.C.§300g-1.

86. Ibid., 100 Stat. 647, 42 U.S.C.§300g-3.

87. Safe Drinking Water Amendments of 1996, 100 Stat. 1613, 42 U.S.C.§300f.

88. Ibid., 100 Stat. 1615, 42 U.S.C.§300f(7).

89. Ibid., 110 Stat. 1627, 42 U.S.C.§300g-1(b)(12).

90. Ibid., 110 Stat. 1641-42, 42 U.S.C.§300f(7).

91. "Governor Pataki, Mayor Giuliani of New York City, EPA, and Upstate Communities Announce a Watershed Agreement," news release issued by the office of Governor George E. Pataki, Albany, New York, November 2, 1995.

92. Public Health Security and Bioterrorism Preparedness and Response Act of 2002, 116 Stat. 682, 42 U.S.C.§300i-2.

93. Robert M. Clark and J. A. Coyle, "Measuring and Modeling Variations in Distribution System Water Quality," *Journal of the American Water Works Association* 2 (1990): 46.

94. Charles Duhigg, "Millions in U.S. Drink Dirty Water, Records Say," *New York Times* (December 8, 2009): 1, A3.

95. *Providing Safe Drinking Water in America: 2009 National Public Water Systems Compliance Report* (Washington, DC: U.S. Environmental Protection Agency, 2011): 1.

96. Ibid., 7.

97. Ibid., 9.

98. *Drinking Water: Unreliable State Data Limit EPA's Ability to Target Enforcement Priorities and Communicate Water Systems' Performance* (Washington, DC: U.S. Government Accountability Office, 2010) [GAO-11-381].

99. *Safe Drinking Water Act: Improvements in Implementation Are Needed to Better Assure the Public of Safe Drinking Water* (Washington, DC: U.S. Government Accountability Office, 2011): 2 [GA0-11-803T].

100. Ibid., 7.

101. Ibid., 19.

CHAPTER 3

1. Consult Arnold W. Reitze Jr., "The Legislative History of U.S. Air Pollution Control." *Houston Law Review* 36 (Fall 1999): 679–741.

2. *Massachusetts Laws of 1910*, chapter 651.

3. United States Public Health Service, *Air Pollution in Donora, PA* (Washington, DC: U.S. Government Printing Office, 1949).

4. Charles O. Jones, *Clean Air: The Policies and Politics of Pollution Control* (Pittsburgh: University of Pittsburgh Press, 1975).

5. Air Control Act of 1955, 69 Stat. 322, 42 U.S.C.§1857.

6. Clean Air Act of 1963, 77 Stat. 372, 42 U.S.C.§1857

7. Ibid.

8. Motor Vehicle Pollution Control Act of 1965, 79 Stat. 992, 42 U.S.C.§1857f-1 (1965).

9. Air Quality Act of 1967, 81 Stat. 485, 42 U.S.C.§1857.

10. *Clean Air Act: Historical Information on EPA's Process for Reviewing California Waiver Requests and Making Waiver Determinations* (Washington, DC: U.S. Government Accountability Office, 2009): 4 [GAO-09-249R].

11. David M. Konisky and Neal D. Woods, "Exporting Air Pollution? Regulatory Enforcement and Environmental Free Riding in the United States," *Political Research Quarterly* 63, no. 4, (2010): 774.

12. Ibid., 779.

13. Clean Air Act Amendments of 1970, 84 Stat. 1676, 42 U.S.C.§1857.

14. Ibid., 84 Stat. 1678, 42 U.S.C.§1857c-2, d–f.

15. *Environmental Quality: The Fourth Annual Report of the Council on Environmental Quality* (Washington, DC: U.S. Government Printing Office, 1973):155.

16. Heidi G. Robertson, "If Your Grandfather Could Pollute, So Can You: Environmental 'Grandfather Clauses' and Their Role in Environmental Equity," *Catholic University Law Review* 45 (1995): 131–79.

17. Bruce R. Huber, "Transition Policy in Environmental Law," *Harvard Environmental Law Review* 35 (2011): 93.

18. Clean Air Amendments of 1970, 84 Stat. 1684.

19. 39 *Federal Register* 8271(1974).

20. *Sierra Club v. Ruckelshaus*, 344 F. Supp.253 (District of Columbia, 1972).

21. *Fri v. Sierra Club*, 412 U.S. 541, 93 S.Ct. 2770 (1973).

22. Tom Tietenberg, "Cap-and-Trade: Evolution of an Economic Idea." *Agricultural and Resource Economics Review* 39 (October 2010): 361.

23. Albert C. Hyde, "The Politics of Environmental Decision Making: the Non-Degradation Issue." Ph.D. Dissertation, Graduate School of Public Affairs, State University of New York at Albany, 1980.

24. 42 *Federal Register* 57460 (November 2, 1977).

25. Hyde, "The Politics of Environmental Decision Making," 261.

26. Clean Air Act Amendments of 1977, 91 Stat. 722, 42 U.S.C.§7424.

27. Patricia M. Crotty, "The New Federalism Game: Primacy Implementation of Environmental Policy," *Publius: The Journal of Federalism* 17 (Spring 1987): 53–67. See also Joseph F. Zimmerman, "The Role of the State Legislature in Air Pollution Abatement," *Suffolk University Law Review* 5 (Spring 1971): 850–77.

28. Grahma Zorn, "Prevention of Significant Deterioration and Its Routine Maintenance Exception: The Definition of Routine, Past, Present, and Future," *Vermont Law Review* 33 (2009): 800.

29. 70 *Federal Register* 25, 162 (2005).

30. *North Carolina v. EPA*, 550 F.3d. 1176 (D.C. Cir. 2008).

31. Clean Air Act Amendments of 1990, 104 Stat. 2399, 42 U.S.C.§750a.

32. Ibid., 104 Stat. 2419, 42 U.S.C.§7506a. See also the U.S. Environmental Protection Agency Rule to Reduce Interstate Transport of Fine Particulate Matter and Ozone, 70 *Federal Register* 25, 162 (May 12, 2005).

33. Joseph F. Zimmerman, *Interstate Cooperation: Compacts and Administrative Agreements* (Westport, CT: Praeger Publishers, 2002): 176–77 and 218.

34. Harry Moren, "The Difficulty of Fencing in Interstate Emissions: EPA's Clean Air Interstate Rule Fails to Make Good Neighbors," *Ecology Law Quarterly* 35 (2009): 533.

35. Clean Air Act Amendments of 1990, 104 Stat. 2529, 42 U.S.C.§7507.

36. Ibid., 104 Stat. 2589, 42 U.S.C.§7651b.

37. *EPA's Acid Rain Program: Results of Phase 1, Outlook for Phase II* (Washington, DC: U.S. Environmental Protection Agency, 2001): 2.

38. *Economic Report of the President* (Washington, DC: U.S. Government Printing Office, 2002): 235.

39. Gabriel Chan, Robert Stavins, Robert Stowe, and Richard Sweeney, "The SO2 Allowance-Trading System and the Clean Air Act Amendments of 1990: Reflections on 20 years of Policy Innovation," *National Tax Journal* 65 (June 2012): 447.

40. Elizabeth Benjamin, "New York Task Force Calls for Sharp Reduction of Carbon Dioxide Emissions," *Times Union* (Albany, NY) (January 10, 2003): 1.

41. The member states are Connecticut, Delaware, Maine, Maryland, Massachusetts, New Hampshire, New Jersey, New York, Rhode Island, and Vermont.

42. *Virginia v. Tennessee*, 148 U.S. 503 at 520, 13 S.Ct. 728 at 735 (1893). Consult Joseph F. Zimmerman, *Horizontal Federalism: Interstate Relations* (Albany: State University of New York Press, 2011): 33–61.

43. Kate Galbraith, "Northeast States Hold Second Carbon Auction," *New York Times* (December 17, 2008): 1.

44. Felicity Barringer, "California Adopts Limits on Greenhouse Gases," *New York Times* (October 21, 2011): A25.

45. Consult Joseph F. Zimmerman, *Interstate Disputes: The Supreme Court's Original Jurisdiction* (Albany: State University of New York Press, 2006).

46. Ibid., 30–34.

47. Consult Joseph F. Zimmerman, *Interstate Cooperation: Compacts and Administrative Agreements* (Albany: State University of New York Press, 2012).

48. *Texas v. Florida*, 306 U.S. 398 at 428, 55 S.Ct. 563 at 577 (1939).

49. Consult Zimmerman, *Interstate Disputes: The Supreme Court's Original Jurisdiction.*

50. *Virginia v. West Virginia*, 246 U.S. 565 at 601–05, 38 S.Ct. 400 at 405–08 (1918).

51. David M. Konisky and Neal D. Woods, "Exporting Air Pollution? Regulatory Enforcement and Environmental Free Riding in the United States," *Political Research Quarterly* 63, no. 4 (2010): 771–82.

52. Clean Air Act, 42 U.S.C.§7410(a)(2)(D)i)(I).

53. "Federal Implementation Plans: Interstate Transport of Fine Particulate Matter and Ozone and Corrections of SIP Approvals," 76 Fed. Reg. 48, 208 (2011). Codified at 40 C.F.R. parts 51, 52, 72, 78, 210–11.

54. EME Hoover City Generation, L.B. v. EPA, 696 F.3d 7 at 19 (2012).

55. 68 Federal Register 52922 (2003).

56. Massachusetts v. Environmental Protection Agency, 415 F.3d 50 (DC Cir., 2005).

57. Massachusetts v. Environmental Protection Agency, 549 U.S. 497, 127 S.Ct. 1438 (2007). See also Jonathan Miller, "Double Absurdity: Regulating Greenhouse Gas Under the Clean Air Act," Houston Law Review 47, no. 5 (2011): 1390–420.

58. 74 Federal Register 66496 et seq. (December 15, 2009).

59. Whitman v. American Trucking Associations, 531 U.S. 457, 121 S.Ct. 903 (2001).

60. Cass R. Sunstein, "Is the Clean Air Act Constitutional?" Michigan Law Review 98 (November 1999): 318.

61. The Benefits and Costs of the Clean Air Act 1990 to 2010 (Washington, DC: U.S. Environmental Protection Agency, 1999.

62. Clean Air Act: EPA Has Completed Most of the Actions Required by the 1990 Amendments, But Many Were Completed Late (Washington, DC: U.S. Government Accountability Office, 2005): 1 [GAO-05-613].

63. The Benefits and Cost of the Clean Air Act 1970 to 1990, and The Benefits and Costs of the Clean Air Act 1990 to 2010 (Washington, DC: U.S. Environmental Protection Agency, 1999).

64. Alan Krupnick and Richard Morgenstern, "The Future of Benefit-Cost Analyses of the Clean Air Act," Annual Review Public Health 23 (2001): 430–31.

65. Ibid., 445.

66. Christopher T. Giovinazzo, "Defending Overstatement: The Symbolic Clean Air Act and Carbon Dioxide," Harvard Environmental Law Review 30 (2006): 162.

67. Michael Greenstone, "Did the Clean Air Act Cause the Remarkable Decline in Sulfur Dioxide Concentrations?" Journal of Environmental Economics and Management 47 (2004): 609.

68. William W. Buzbee, "Clean Air Act Dynamism and Disappointments: Lessons for Climate Legislation to Prompt Innovation and Discourage Inertia," Washington University Journal of Law and Policy 32 (2010): 44–45.

69. Ibid., 76.

70. Tietenberg, "Cap-and-Trade," 365.

71. Carbon Emission (CO) National Emission Trends (Short Tons) (Washington, DC: U.S. Environmental Protection Agency, 2011).

72. "Administrator Lisa P. Jackson, Testimony Before the U.S. House Subcommittee on Oversight and Investigations, a news release issued by the U.S. Environmental Protection Administration, September 22, 2011.

73. "EPA Announces Most Areas Meet Air Quality Standards for Lead." News release issued by the U.S. Environmental Protection Agency, November 9, 2011.

74. Craig N. Oren, "Is the Clean Air Act at a Crossroads? *Environmental Law* 40 (2010): 1238.

75. Douglas R. Williams, "Toward Regional Governance in Environmental Laws," *Akron Law Review* 46.

76. Ibid. (2013): 1090.

CHAPTER 4

1. *Paul v. Virginia*, 75 U.S. 168, 8 Wallace 168 (1868).

2. *United States v. South Eastern Underwriters Association*, 322 U.S. 533, 64 S.Ct. 1162 (1944).

3. McCarran-Ferguson Act of 1945, 59 Stat. 33, 15 U.S.C. §1011.

4. Gramm-Leach-Bliley Financial Modernization Act of 1999, 113 Stat. 1353, 15 U.S.C.§6701.

5. Ibid., 113 Stat. 1422, 15 U.S.C. §6751.

6. "Members Certify GLBA Reciprocity Requirement Met," a news release issued by the National Association of Insurance Commissioners, September 11, 2002.

7. E-Mail message from Associate Counsel John Bauer of the National Association of Insurance Commissioners, August 12, 2002.

8. *Financial Regulation Standards and Accreditation Program* (Kansas City: National Association of Insurance Commissioners, 2000).

9. Richard J. Hillman, *Efforts to Streamline Key Licensing and Approval Processes Face Challenges* (Washington, DC: U.S. General Accounting Office, 2002).

10. Atomic Energy Act of 1946, 60 Stat. 755, 42 U.S.C.§2011.

11. Atomic Energy Act of 1954, 68 Stat. 919, 42 U.S.C.§841.

12. Joseph F. Zimmerman, "Zoning for Atomic Energy Uses," *Zoning Digest* 16 (1964): 161–69.

13. See Joseph F. Zimmerman, *Cities versus Atoms*," *National Civic Review* 50 (April 1961):1–7.

14. Atomic Energy Act of 1959, 73 Stat. 688, 42 U.S.C.§2021.

15. United States Grain Standards Act of 1968, 82 Stat. 769, 7 U.S.C.§71.

16. Federal Railroad Safety Act of 1970, 84 Stat. 971, 45 U.S.C.§431.

17. Hazardous Materials Transportation Act Amendments of 1976, 90 Stat. 2068, 49 U.S.C. Appendix §1805c.

18. Hazardous and Solid Waste Amendments of 1984, 98 Stat. 3256, 42 U.S.C.§6901.

19. Age Discrimination in Employment Amendments of 1986, 100 Stat. 3342, 29 U.S.C.§623.

20. Oil Pollution Act of 1990, 104 Stat. 506, 33 U.S.C.§2719.

21. Anti Car Theft Act of 1992, 106 Stat. 3384, 18 U.S.C.§2119.

22. Antiterrorism and Effective Death Penalty Act of 1996, 100 Stat 1276, 8 U.S.C.§1252c.

23. Coast Guard and Marine Transportation Act of 2004, 118 Stat. 1978, 46 U.S.C.§70119(a).

24. Magnuson-Stevens Fishery Conservation and Management Reauthorization Act of 2006, 120 Stat. 3596, 16 U.S.C.§1861(b)(1)(A)(3).

25. Nutrition Labeling and Education Act of 1920, 41 Stat. 2362, 21 U.S.C.§337(b)(1).

26. Federal Environmental Pesticide Control Act of 1972, 86 Stat. 996, 7 U.S.C.§136u.

27. Consumer Product Safety Improvement Act of 1990, 104 Stat. 3142, 15 U.S.C.§§1184(a), 1264.

28. Oil Pollution Act of 1990, 104 Stat. 506, 33 U.S.C.§2719.

29. Telephone Consumer Protection Act of 1991, 105 Stat. 2400, 47 U.S.C.§227(f).

30. Telephone Disclosure and Dispute Resolution Act of 1992, 106 Stat. 4190, 15 U.S.C.§5712.

31. Telemarketing and Consumer Fraud and Abuse Prevention Act of 1994, 108 Stat. 1548, 15 U.S.C.§6103.

32. Capital Markets Efficiency Act of 1996, 110 Stat. 3419, 15 U.S.C.§77r(c).

33. Consumer Credit Report Reform Act of 1996, 110 Stat. 3009–451 to 3009–453, 15 U.S.C.§1681s(2)(b–c).

34. Omnibus Consolidated Appropriations Act for Fiscal Year 1997, 110 Stat. 3009, 15 U.S.C.§1681s(e)(1).

35. Children Online Privacy Protection Act of 1998, 112 Stat. 2681, 15 U.S.C.§6504.

36. Twenty-First Amendment Enforcement Act of 2000, 114 Stat. 1546, 27 U.S.C.§122a(b)(1–2).

37. Controlling the Assault of Non-Solicited Pornography and Marketing Act of 2003, 117 Stat. 2712, 15 U.S.C.§7706.

38. Junk Fax Prevention Act of 2005, 119 Stat. 359, 49 U.S.C.§609.

39. Restore Online Shoppers Confidence Act of 2010, 124 Stat. 3621, 15 U.S.C.§8404.

CHAPTER 5

1. Consult Joseph F. Zimmerman, *Congressional Preemption: Regulatory Federalism* (Albany: State University of New York Press, 2005).

2. Johnson Act of 1951, 64 Stat. 1134, 15 U.S.C.§1172(a).

3. Coastal Zone Management Act of 1972, 86 Stat. 1280, 16 U.S.C. §1451, and Nuclear Waste Policy Act of 1982, 96 Stat. 2217, 42 U.S.C. §10135.

4. Toxic Substances Control Act of 1976, 90 Stat. 2003, 15 U.S.C.§2601.

5. Port and Tanker Safety Act of 1978, 92 Stat. 1471, 33 U.S.C.§214. This act has been replaced by 46 U.S.C.§§7106, 7109.

6. Nuclear Waste Policy Act of 1982, 96 Stat. 2217, 42 U.S.C.§10125.

7. Omnibus Budget Reconciliation Act of 1988, 98 Stat. 437, 23 U.S.C.§158.

8. Yucca Mountain High Level Radioactive Waste Site Act of 2002, 116 Stat. 735, 42 U.S.C.§10135.

9. Coast Guard Authorization Act of 1984, 98 Stat. 2862, 46 U.S.C.§2302.

10. Atlantic Striped Bass Conservation Act Amendments of 1986, 100 Stat. 989, 16 U.S.C.§1851.

11. Abandoned Shipwreck Act of 1987, 102 Stat. 432, 43 U.S.C.§2101.

12. Riegle-Neal Interstate Banking and Branching Efficiency Act of 1994, 108 Stat. 2343, 12 U.S.C.§1831u.

13. Ibid., 108 Stat. 2352, 12 U.S.C.§36g.

14. An Act to Revise and Codify Title 49, United States Code, 108 Stat. 272, 49 U.S.C.§31705 (1994).

15. Consult Joseph F. Zimmerman, *Interstate Cooperation: Compacts and Administrative Agreements* (Westport, CT: Praeger Publishers, 2002): 165, 190–92.

16. *Electronic Signatures in Global and National Commerce Act of 2000*, 114 Stat. 464, 15 U.S.C.§7001.

17. *Hotel and Motel Fire Safety Act of 1990*, 104 Stat. 747, 5 U.S.C.§5701. See also the Federal *Fire Prevention and Control Act of 1974*, 88 Stat. 1535, 15 U.S.C.§2224.

18. *Muhammad Ali Boxing Reform Act of 2000*, 114 Stat. 322, 15 U.S.C §6301.

19. Ibid., 114 Stat. 323, 15 U.S.C.§6307c.

20. Ibid.

21. Felix Frankfurter and James M. Landis, "The Compact Clause of the Constitution—A Study in Interstate Adjustments," *Yale Law Journal* 34 (May 1925): 687–88.

22. Consult Zimmerman, *Interstate Cooperation: Compacts and Administrative Agreements*.

CHAPTER 6

1. Max M. Farrand, ed. *The Records of the Constitutional Convention of 1787*, vol. II (New Haven: Yale University Press, 1966): 27.

2. Copyright Act of 1790 1 Stat. 124, 7 U.S.C.§301, Patent Act of 1790, 1 Stat. 109, 35 U.S.C.§1.

3. Voting Rights Act of 1965, 79 Stat. 437, 42 U.S.C.§1973.

4. Atlantic Striped Bass Conservation Act Amendments of 1986, 100 Stat. 989, 16 U.S.C.§1851, Gramm-Leach-Bliley Financial Modernization Act of 1999, 113 Stat. 1423, 15 U.S.C.§6751, and Energy Policy Act of 2005, 119 Stat. 947, 16 U.S.C.§824p.

5. Voting Rights Act of 1965, 79 Stat. 437, 42 U.S.C.§1973.

6. Voting Rights Act Amendments of 1975, 89 Stat. 438, 42 U.S.C.§1973.

7. Voting Rights Language Assistance Act of 1992, 106 Stat. 941, 21 U.S.C.§1071.

8. *City of Petersburg v. United States*, 354 F. Supp.1021 (D.C.C. 1972), affirmed, 410 U.S. 962 (1973); *White v. Register*, 412 U.S. 755, 93 S.Ct. 2332 (1973); and *City of Richmond v. United States*, 422 U.S. 358, 95 S.Ct. 2296 (1975).

9. For a review of the act, consult Stephen Ansolabehere, Nathaniel Persily, and Charles Stewart III, "Race, Region, and Vote Choices in the 2008 Election: Implications for the Future of the Voting Rights Act," *Harvard Law Review* 123 (2010): 1386–436.

10. See, generally, Richard S. Childs, *The First Fifty Years of the Council-Manager Form of Government* (New York: National Municipal League, 1965).

11. Consult Woodrow W. Wilson and Richard S. Childs, *The Short Ballot* (New York: National Short Ballot Association, 1916).

12. See, for example, *Perry v. Opelousas*, 515 F.2d 639 (5th Cir. 1975); *Turner v. McKeithen*, 490 F.2d 191 (5th Cir.1973); and *Zimmer v. McKeithen*, 485 F.2d 1297 (5th Cir. 1973) (enbanc).

13. The covered units were Bronx, Kings, and New York counties. The Voting Rights Act Amendments of 1970—84 Stat. 314, 42 U.S.C.§1973—advanced the date to 1968, at which certain prerequisites had to exist to subject a local government to the act's provisions.

14. *National Association for the Advancement of Colored People v. New York*, 413 U.S. 345, 93 S.Ct. 2591 (1973).

15. See *New York v. United States*, 419 U.S. 888, 95 S.Ct. 166 (1974).

16. Although the New York State Legislature had redistricted the state in 1972, the U.S. Attorney General rejected that plan, which constituted a change to an electoral system requiring approval under the Voting Rights Act.

17. *United Jewish Organizations, Incorporated v. Carey*, 430 U.S. 144 at 152–53, 97 S.Ct. 996 at 1003 (1976).

18. Linda Greenhouse, "Hasidic Jews Are Called 'Victims of a Racial Gerrymander' at Hearing on Suit," *New York Times* (June 21, 1974): 19.

19. "U.S. Accepts Plan on Districts Here," *New York Times* (July 2, 1974): 24.

20. See *United Jewish Organizations, Incorporated v. Wilson*, 430 U.S. 144 at 161, note 19, 97 S.Ct. 996 at 1007 (1976).

21. *United Jewish Organizations, Incorporated v. Wilson*, 377 F. Supp.1164 at 1165–166 (1974).

22. *United Jewish Organizations, Incorporated v. Wilson*, 510 F.2d 512 at 523 (D.C. Cir 1975).

23. Ibid. at 521.

24. *United Jewish Organization, Incorporated v. Wilson*, 430 U.S. 14, 97 S.Ct. 996 (1977).

25. Ibid., at 156, 159–60, 161.

26. Ibid., at 170–71.

27. *Gomillion v. Lightfoot* 364 U.S. 339, 81 S.Ct. 125 (1960), and *Wright v. Rockefeller*, 376 U.S. 52, 84 S.Ct. 603 (1964).

28. *Wright v. Rockefeller*, 376 U.S. 52 at 67, 84 S.Ct. 603 at 611.

29. *United Jewish Organizations, Incorporated v. Wilson*, 430 U.S. 144 at 186–87, 97 S.Ct. 996 at 1020–021 (1977).

30. Ibid., 430 U.S. 144 at 186, 97 S.Ct. 996 at 1020.

31. Ibid., Puerto Rican groups claimed the 1974 redistricting plan discriminated against them.

32. Ibid., 430 U.S. 144 at 166, 97 S.Ct. 996 at 1010.

33. Ibid., 430 U.S. at 169, 97 S.Ct. 996 at 1011.

34. Arguably, a minority group could have greater political influence by providing the swing vote in many districts than it would have by possessing a clear majority in a few districts. See *Wright v. Rockefeller*, 376 U.S. 52, 84 S.Ct. 603 (1974). A black petitioner and a black intervener disagreed as to the relative effectiveness of these two approaches.

35. *United Jewish Organization v. Wilson*, 430 U.S. 144 at 186.

36. Ibid., at 162.

37. Ibid., at 185 (Chief Justice Burger dissenting).

38. Consult Joseph F. Zimmerman, *The Federated City: Community Control in Large Cities* (New York: St. Martin's Press, 1972): 72–74 and 76.

39. *New York City Charter*, chapter 2, §22 (1963).

40. *Avery v. Midland County, Texas et al.*, 390 U.S. 474, 88 S.Ct. 114 (1968).

41. *Northwest Austin Municipal Utility District No. One v. Holder*, 557 U.S. 193 at 201, 129 S.Ct. 2504 at 2512 (2009).

42. Ibid. at 2516.

43. Ibid. at 2517.

44. Atlantic States Marine Fisheries Compact, 56 Stat. 267 (1942).

45. *69th Annual Report of the Atlantic States Marine Fisheries Commission* (Arlington, VA: 2011).

46. Atlantic Striped Bass Conservation Act Amendments of 1986, 100 Stat. 989, 16 U.S.C.§1851.

47. Joseph A. Farside Jr., "Atlantic States Marine Fishery Commission: Getting a Grip on Slippery Fisheries Management," *Roger Williams University Law Review* 11 (Fall 2005): 241.

48. Atlantic Coastal Fisheries Cooperative Fisheries Management Act of 1993, 107 Stat. 2447, 16 U.S.C.§5101(a)(3). This act is contained in the *Coast Guard Authorization Act of 1993*.

49. Ibid., 107 Stat. 2447, 16 U.S.C.§§5101–108.

50. *Annual Report* (Washington, DC: Atlantic States Marine Fisheries Commission, 2010): 9.

51. *United States v. South-Eastern Underwriters Association et al.*, 332 U.S. 533, 64 S.Ct. 3162 (1944).

52. McCarran-Ferguson Act of 1945, 59 Stat. 33, 15 U.S.C.§1011. Consult also The Act of July 2, 1890. (Sherman Act), 26 Stat. 209, 15 U.S.C.§1; Clayton Antitrust Act of 1914, 38 Stat. 370, 15 U.S.C.§12; and Federal Trade Commission Act of 1914, 38 Stat. 717, 15 U.S.C.§41.

53. Gramm-Leach-Bliley Financial Modernization Act of 1999, 113 Stat. 1338, 12 U.S.C.§1811.

54. Ibid., 113 Stat. 1422, 15 U.S.C.§6751.

55. Ibid., 113 Stat. 1353, 15 U.S.C.§6701.

56. Energy Policy Act of 2005, 119 Stat. 947, 16 U.S.C.§824p.

57. Ibid., 16 U.S.C.§824p(b).

58. Ibid., 16 U.S.C.§824p(i)(1).

59. E-Mail message from Mark Hershfield of the Office of External Affairs of the Federal Energy Regulatory Commission, March 31, 2011.

CHAPTER 7

1. *The Federalist Papers* (New York: New American Library, 1961): 119.

2. M. J. C. Vile, *The Structure of American Federalism* (Oxford: Oxford University Press, 1961): 35.

3. Jane Perry Clark, "Interdependent Federal and State Law as a Form of Federal-State Cooperation," *Iowa Law Review* 23 (1936): 539.

4. Americans with Disabilities Act of 1990, 104 Stat. 327, 42 U.S.C.§12101.

5. Daniel J. Elazar, *American Federalism: A View from the States*, 3rd ed. (New York: Harper & Row, 1984).

6. Letter to author from Director Daniel J. Elazar of Temple University's Center for the Study of Federalism, December 7, 1992.

7. U.S. Constitution, art. I, §10.

8. John R. Koza, Barry F. Fadem, Mark Grueskin, Michael S. Mandell, Robert Richie, and Joseph F. Zimmerman, *Every Vote Equal: A State-Based Plan for Electing the President by National Popular Vote*, 4th ed. (Los Altos, CA: National Popular Vote Press, 2013).

9. Felix Frankfurter and Charles Landis, "The Commerce Clause of the Constitution—A Study in Interstate Adjustments," *Yale Law Journal* 34 (1925): 688.

10. Delaware River Basin Compact (Delaware, New Jersey, New York, and Pennsylvania), 75 Stat. 688 (1962).

11. Consult Joseph F. Zimmerman, *Horizontal Federalism: Interstate Relations* (Albany: State University of New York Press, 2011).

12. Airline Deregulation Act of 1978, 92 Stat. 1708, 49 U.S.C.§1305.

13. Richard Perz-Pena and Patrick McGeehan, "Assault on Wall St. Misdeeds Raises Spitzer's U.S. Profile," *New York Times* (November 4, 2002): 1, B6.

14. *Regulatory Federalism: Policy, Process, Impact, and Reform* (Washington, DC: U.S. Advisory Commission on Intergovernmental Relations, 1992).

15. Ibid., 139.

16. Ibid., 139–44.

17. Robert L. Glickman, "From Cooperative to Inoperative Federalism: The Perverse Mutation of Environmental Law and Policy," *Wake Forest Law Review* 41 (2006): 777.

Bibliography

BOOKS

Anderson, William. *Intergovernmental Relations in Review*. Minneapolis: University of Minnesota Press, 1960.

Bailey, Thomas A. *The American Pageant: A History of the Republic*, 3rd ed. Boston: D. C. Heath, 1967.

Calhoun, John C. *Disquisition on Government*. New York: Political Science Classics, 1948.

Clark, Jane P. *The Rise of a New Federalism: Federal-State Cooperation in the United States*. New York: Columbia University Press, 1938.

Childs, Richard S. *The First Fifty Years of the Council-Manager Form of Municipal Government*. New York: National Municipal League, 1965.

Conlan, Timothy. *From New Federalism to Devolution: Twenty-Five Years of Intergovernmental Reform*. Washington, DC: Brookings Institution, 1998.

Corwin, Edward S. *The Commerce Power Versus States' Rights*. Princeton: Princeton University Press, 1936.

———. *National Supremacy: Treaty Power vs. State Power*. New York: Henry Holt, 1913.

Elazar, Daniel J. *American Federalism: A View from the States*, 3rd ed. New York: Harper & Row, 1984.

———. *The American Partnership: Intergovernmental Cooperation in the Nineteenth Century*. Chicago: University of Chicago Press, 1962.

———. *Exploring Federalism*. Tuscaloosa: University of Alabama Press, 1987.

Elliot, Jonathan, ed. *The Debates in the Several State Conventions on the Adoption of the Federal Constitution*, 2nd ed., 5 vols. Philadelphia: J. P. Lippincott & Company, 1876.

Epstein, David F. *The Political Theory of the Federalist*. Chicago: University of Chicago Press, 1984.

Farrand, Max. *The Fathers of the Constitution*. New Haven: Yale University Press, 1921.

———. ed. *The Records of the Federal Constitution of 1787*. New Haven: Yale University Press, 1956.

Feenberg, Daniel and Edwin S. Mills. *Measuring the Benefits of Water Pollution Abatement*. New York: Academic Press, 1980.

Ford, Paul L. *The Writings of Thomas Jefferson*, vol. 9. New York: G. P. Putnam, 1898.

Frankfurter, Felix. *The Commerce Clause Under Marshall, Taney, and Waite*. Chapel Hill: University of North Carolina Press, 1937.

Friedich, Carl J. *Trends of Federalism in Theory and Practice*. New York: Frederick A. Praeger, 1968.

Graves, W. Brooke. *American Intergovernmental Relations: Their Origins, Historical Development, and Current Status*. New York: Charles Scribner's Sons, 1964.

Grodzins, Morton. *The American System: A New View of Government in the United States*. Chicago: Rand McNally & Company, 1966.

Hamilton, Alexander, James Madison, and John Jay. *The Federalist Papers*. New York: New American Library 1961.

Hofstadter, Richard, William Miller, and Daniel Aaron. *The American Republic*. Englewood Cliffs, NJ: Prentice-Hall Incorporated, 1959.

Hunt, Gaillard, ed. *The Writings of James Madison*. New York: G. P. Putnam's Sons, 1901.

Jensen, Merrill. *The Articles of Confederation*. Madison: University of Wisconsin Press, 1940.

Kaminski, John P., and Gaspare J. Saladmo. *The Documentary History of the Ratification of the Constitution*. Madison: State Historical Society of Wisconsin, 1981.

Ketcham, Ralph., ed. *The Anti-Federalist Papers and the Constitutional Convention Debates*. New York: New American Library, 1986.

Kettl, Donald F. *The Regulation of American Federalism*. Baton Rouge: Louisiana State University Press, 1983.

Laski, Harold J. *The American Democracy: A Commentary and an Interpretation*. New York: Viking Press, 1948.

Leach, Richard H. *American Federalism*. New York: W. W. Norton Company, 1970.

MacMahon, Arthur W., ed. *Federalism: Mature and Emergent*. Garden City, NY: Doubleday and Company, 1955.

Madison, James. *Journal of the Federal Convention*. Chicago: Albert, Scott & Company, 1893.

Main, Jackson T. *The Antifederalists: Critics of the Constitution 1781–1788*. Chapel Hill: University of North Carolina Press, 1961.

Morgan, Iwan W. and Phillip J. Davies, eds. *The Federal Nation: Perspectives on American Federalism*. New York: Palgrave-Macmillan, 2008.

Morley, Felix. *Freedom and Federalism*. Chicago: Henry Regnery Company, 1959.

Nagle, Robert F. *The Implosion of American Federalism*. New York: Oxford University Press, 2002.

O'Reilly, James T. *Federal Preemption of State and Local Law: Legislation, Regulation, and Litigation*. Chicago: Section on Administrative law and Regulatory Practice, American Bar Association, 2006.

Riker, William H. *Federalism: Origin, Operation, Significance*. Boston: Little, Brown and Company, 1964.

Section of Natural Resources, Energy, and Environmental Law. *The Clean Air Act Amendments of 1990: Where EPA and the States Are Going*. Chicago: American Bar Association, 1988.

Storing, Herbert, J. *What the Anti-Federalists Were For*. Chicago: University of Chicago Press, 1981.

Story, Joseph. *Commentaries on the Constitution of the United States*. Boston: Hilliard, Gray, and Company, 1833.

Tiratsoo, J. N. H., ed. *Pipeline Pegging Technology*, 2nd ed. Woburn, MA: Butterworth-Heinemann, 1999.

Vile, M. J. C. *The Structure of American Federalism*. Oxford: Oxford University Press, 1961.

Walker, Robert H., ed. *The Reform Spirit in America: A Documentation of Reform in the American Republic*. New York: G. P. Putnam, 1976.

Warren, Charles. *Congress, the Constitution, and the Supreme Court*. Boston: Little, Brown and Company, 1925.

Woodrow W. Wilson and Richard S. Childs. *The National Short Ballot*. New York: National Short Ballot Association, 1916.

Wright, Deil S. *Understanding Intergovernmental Relations*, 3rd ed. Pacific Grove, CA: Brooks/Cole Publishing, 1988.

Zimmerman, Joseph F. *Congress: Facilitator of State Action*. Albany: State University of New York Press, 2010.

———. *Congressional Preemption: Regulatory Federalism*. Albany: State University of New York Press, 2005.

———. *Contemporary American Federalism: The Growth of National Power*. Albany: State University of New York Press, 2008.

———. *Federal Preemption: The Silent Revolution*. Ames: Iowa State University Press, 1991.

———. *The Federated City: Community Control in Large Cities*. New York: St. Martin's Press, 1972.

———. *Interstate Cooperation: Compacts and Administrative Agreements*, 2nd ed. Albany: State University of New York Press, 2012.

———. *Interstate Disputes: The Supreme Court's Original Jurisdiction*. Albany: State University of New York Press, 2006.

———. *Interstate Economic Relations*. Albany: State University of New York Press, 2004.

———. *Interstate Water Compacts: Intergovernmental Efforts to Manage America's Water Resources*. Albany: State University of New York Press, 2012.

———. *The Silence of Congress: State Taxation of Interstate Commerce*. Albany: State University of New York Press, 2007.

———. *State-Local Governmental Interactions*. Albany: State University of New York Press, 2012.

———. *Unifying the Nation: Article IV of the United States Constitution*. Albany: State University of New York Press, 2015.

PUBLIC DOCUMENTS

American Federalism: Toward a More Effective Partnership. Washington, DC: U.S. Advisory Commission on Intergovernmental Relations, 1975.

Annual Report. Washington, DC: Atlantic States Marine Fisheries Commission, 2010.

Boyd, Eugene. *American Federalism: 1776–1995.* Washington, DC: Congressional Research Service, 1995.

Categorical Grants: Their Role and Design. The Intergovernmental Grant System: An Assessment and Proposed Policies. Washington, DC: U.S. Advisory Commission on Intergovernmental Relations, 1978.

Clean Air Act: EPA Has Completed Most of the Actions Required by the 1990 Amendments, but Many Were Completed Late. Washington, DC: U.S. Government Accountability Office, 2005 (GAO-05-613).

Clean Water Act: Longstanding Issues Impact EPA's and States' Enforcement Efforts. Washington, DC: U.S. Government Accountability Office, 2009 (GAO-10-165T).

Commission on Intergovernmental Relations: A Report to the President for Transmittal to the Congress. Washington, DC: U.S. Government Printing Office, 1955.

Community Development Block Grants: Program Offers Recipients Flexibility but Oversight Can Be Improved. Washington, DC: U.S. Government Accountability Office, 2006.

Congressional Preemption of State Laws and Regulations: A Report Prepared for Representative Henry A. Waxman. United States House of Representatives Committee on Governmental Reform—Minority State, Special Investigations Division, June 2006.

Copeland, Claudia. *Water Quality: Implementing the Clean Water Act.* Washington, DC: Congressional Research Service, 2006.

———, and Jeffrey Zinn. *Animal Waste Management and the Environment: Background for Current Issues.* Washington, DC: Congressional Research Service, 1998.

Cucitti, Peggy L. *Federal Constraints on State and Local Governments.* Washington, DC: Congressional Budget Office, 1979.

Devolving Federal Program Responsibilities and Revenue Sources to State and Local Governments. Washington, DC: U.S. Advisory Commission on Intergovernmental Relations, 1986.

Drinking Water: Consumer Often Not Well-Informed of Potentially Serious Violations. Washington, DC: U.S. General Accounting Office, 1992 (GAO/RCED-92-135).

Drinking Water: EPA Should Strengthen Ongoing Efforts to Ensure that Consumers Are Protected from Lead Contamination. Washington, DC: U.S. Government Accountability Office, 2006 (GAO-06-148).

Economic Report of the President. Washington, DC: U.S. Government Printing Office, 2002.

Effects of Coal-Mine Drainage on Stream Water Quality in the Allegheny and Monongahela River Basins—Sulfate Transport and Trends. Lemoyne, PA: National Water-Quality Assessment Program, 2000.

EPA's Acid Rain Program: Results of Phase 1, Outlook for Phase II. Washington, DC: U.S. Environmental Protection Agency, 2001.

Federal Water Requirements: Challenges to Estimating the Cost Impact on Local Communities. Washington, DC: U.S. Government Accountability Office, 2005 (GAO-06-151R).

The Federal Influence on State and Local Government Roles in the Federal System. Washington, DC: U.S. Advisory Commission on Intergovernmental Relations, 1981.

Federal Mandates: Few Rules Trigger Unfunded Mandates Reform Act. Washington, DC: United States Government Accountability Office, 2011.

Federal Water Requirements: Challenges to Estimating the Cost Impact on Local Communities. Washington, DC: U.S. Government Accountability Office, 2005 (GAO-06-151R).

Fiscal Balance in the American Federal System. Washington, DC: U.S. Advisory Commission on Intergovernmental Relations, 1967.

Flexibility in the Safe Drinking Water Act. Washington, DC: U.S. General Accounting Office (RCED-96-12R).

Future Investment in Drinking Water and Wastewater Infrastructure. Washington, DC: Congressional Budget Office, 2002.

General Revenue Sharing: An ACIR Evaluation. Washington, DC: U.S. Advisory Commission on Intergovernmental Relations, 1974.

Hardrock Mining: BLM Needs to Better Manage Financial Assurances to Guarantee Coverage of Reclamation Costs. Washington, DC: U.S. Government Accountability Office, 2005 (GAO-05-377).

Improved EPA Guidance and Support Can Help States Develop Standards That Better Target Cleanup Efforts. 2003 (GAO-03-308).

Interstate Tax Competition. Washington, DC: U.S. Advisory Commission on Intergovernmental Relations, 1981.

Key EPA and State Decisions Limited by Inconsistent and Incomplete Data. Washington, DC: U.S. Government Accountability Office, 2000 (GAO/RCED-00-54).

Kilduff, Patrick, John Carmichael, and Robert Latour. *Guide to Fisheries Science and Stock Assessments*. Washington, DC: Atlantic States Marine Fisheries Commission, 2009.

Living Shorelines: Impacts of Erosion Control Strategies on Coastal Habitats. Washington, DC: Atlantic States Marine Fisheries Commission, 2010.

North American Free Trade Agreement: Coordinated Operational Plan Needed to Ensure Mexican Trucks' Compliance with U.S. Standards. Washington, DC: U.S. General Accounting Office, 2002.

Parfomax, Paul W. *BP Alaska North Slope Pipeline Shutdowns: Regulatory Policy Issues*. Washington, DC: Congressional Research Service, 2007.

———. *Keeping America's Pipeline Safe and Secure: Key Issues for Congress*. Washington, DC: Congressional Research Service, 2010.

———. *Pipeline Safety and Security: Federal Programs.* Washington, DC: Congressional Research Service, 2010.

Posner, Paul L. *Federal Assistance: Grant System Continues to Be Highly Fragmented.* Washington, DC: U.S. General Accounting Office, 2003.

———. *Regulatory Programs: Balancing Federal and State Responsibilities for Standard Setting and Implementation.* Washington, DC: U.S. General Accounting Office, 2002.

Regulatory Federalism: Policy, Process, Impact, and Reform. Washington, DC: U.S. Advisory Commission on Intergovernmental Relations, 1984.

Safe Drinking Water Act: Progress and Future Challenges in Implementing the 1996 Amendments. Washington, DC: U.S. General Accounting Office, 1999 (GAO/RCED-99-31).

Sams, James L., III, and Kevin M. Beer. *Effects of Coal-Mine Drainage on Stream Water Quality in the Allegheny and Monongahela River Basins—Sulfate Transport and Trends.* Lemoyne, PA: National Water Quality Assessment Program, 2000.

Sixty-Ninth Annual Report of the Atlantic States Marine Fisheries Commission. Arlington, VA: Atlantic States Marine Fisheries Commission, 2011.

State Taxation of Interstate Mail Order Sales. Washington, DC: U.S. Advisory Commission on Intergovernmental Relations, 1992.

Stenberg, Carl W. *State Involvement in Federal-Local Grant Programs: A Case Study of the "Buying in" Approach.* Washington, DC: U.S. Advisory Commission on Intergovernmental Relations, 1970.

Stephenson, John B. *Federal Water Requirements: Challenges to Estimating the Cost Impact on Local Communities.* Washington, DC: U.S. Government Accountability Office, 2005 (GAO-06-151R).

Surface Coal Mining: Characteristics of Mining in Mountainous Areas of Kentucky and West Virginia. Washington, DC: U.S. Government Accountability Office, 2009 (GAO-10-21).

Surface Coal Mining: Financial Assurances for, and Long-Term Oversight of, Mines with Valley Fills in Four Appalachian States. Washington, DC: U.S. Government Accountability Office, 2010 (GAO-10-206).

Zimmerman, Joseph F. *Federal Preemption of State and Local Authority.* Washington, DC: U.S. Advisory Commission on Intergovernmental Relations, 1990.

———. *Federally Induced Costs Affecting State and Local Governments.* Washington, DC: U.S. Advisory Commission on Intergovernmental Relations, 1994.

———. *Pragmatic Federalism: The Reassignment of Functional Responsibility.* Washington, DC: U.S. Advisory Commission on Intergovernmental Relations, 1976.

Zimmerman, Joseph F., and Sharon Lawrence. *Federal Statutory Preemption of State and Local Authority: History, Inventory, and Issues.* Washington, DC: United States Advisory Commission on Intergovernmental Relations, 1992.

ARTICLES

Adelman, David E., and Kirsten H. Engel. "Adaptive Federalism: The Case Against Reallocating Environmental Regulatory Authority." *Minnesota Law Review* 92 (2008): 1796–850.

Adler, Robert W. "Integrated Approaches to Water Pollution: Lessons from the Clean Air Act." *Harvard Environmental Law Review* 23 (1999): 203–07.

———. "The Two Lost Books in the Water Quality Trilogy: The Elusive Objectives of Physical and Biological Integrity." *Environmental Law* 33 (2003): 29–77.

———. "Resilience, Restoration, and Sustainability: Revisiting the Fundamental Principles of the Clean Water Act." *Journal of Law & Policy* 12 (2010): 129–73.

———. "When Is Two a Crowd? The Impact of Federal Action on State Environmental Regulation." *Harvard Environmental Law Review* 31 (2007): 67–114.

Agranoff, Robert. "Managing Within the Matrix: Do Collaborative Intergovernmental Relations Exist?" *Publius: The Journal of Federalism* 31 (September 2001): 31–56.

Alexander, James R. "State Sovereignty in the Federal System: Constitutional Protections Under the Tenth and Eleventh Amendments." *Publius: The Journal of Federalism* 16 (Spring 1986): 1–15.

Althouse, Ann. "How to Build a Separate Sphere: Federal Courts and State Power." *Harvard Law Review* 100 (May 1987): 1485–538.

Anderson, Scott D. "Watershed Management and Nonpoint Pollution." *Boston College Environmental Affairs Law Review* 26 (1999): 239–86.

Baker, Thomas E. "A Catalogue of Judicial Federalism in the United States." *South Carolina Law Review* 46 (Summer 1995): 835–75.

Barnett, James D. "Cooperation Between the Federal and State Governments." *National Municipal Review* 17 (May 1928): 283–91.

———. "The Delegation of Legislative Power by Congress to the States." *American Political Science Review* 2 (1908): 347–77.

Baybeck, Brady, and William Lowry. "Federalism Outcomes and Ideological Preferences: The U.S. Supreme Court and Preemption Cases." *Publius: The Journal of Federalism* 30 (Summer 2000): 73–97.

Behnke, Jim. "Safety Jurisdiction Over Natural Gas Pipelines." *Energy Law Journal* 19 (1998): 71–118.

Biancardi, Paul, and Lisa M. Bogardus. "From 'Command and Control' to Risk Management: The Evolution of the Federal Natural Gas Pipeline Safety Program." *Energy Law Quarterly* 16 (1995): 461–88

Bork, Robert H., and Daniel E. Troy. "Locating the Boundaries: The Scope of Congress' Power to Regulate Commerce." *Harvard Journal of Law and Public Policy* 25 (Summer 2002): 849–93.

Braden, George B. "Umpire to the Federal System." *University of Chicago Law Review* 10 (October 1942): 27–48.

Briceland, Alan V. "Virginia's Ratification of the U.S. Constitution." *Newsletter* (Institute of Government, University of Virginia) 61 (October 1984): 1–14.

Brilmayer, Lea. "Federalism, State Authority, and the Preemptive Power of International Law." *The Supreme Court Reporter* (1944): 295–343.

Buckley, James L. "The Trouble with Federalism: It Isn't Being Tried." *Commonsense* 1 (Summer 1978): 1–17.

Butler, Henry N., and Jonathan R. Macey. *Yale Law and Policy Review* 14 (1996): 23–66.

Buzbee, William W. "Clean Air Act Dynamism and Disappointments: Lessons for Climate Litigation to Prompt Innovation and Discourage Inertia." *Washington University of Journal of Law and Policy* 32 (2010): 33–77.

Calande, Pauline E. "State Incorporation of Federal Law: A Response to the Demise of Implied Federal Rights of Action." *Yale Law Journal* 94 (April 1985): 1144–163.

Carstens, Anne-Marie. "Lurking in the Shadows of Judicial Process: Special Masters in the Supreme Court's Original Jurisdiction Cases." *Minnesota Law Review* 86 (February 2002): 625–704.

Cauley, Richard F. "Constitutionality of Warrantless Environmental Inspections." *Columbia Journal of Environmental Law* 15 (1990): 83–97.

Clark, Jane Perry. "Interdependent Federal and State Law as a Form of Federal-State Cooperation." *Iowa Law Review* 23 (1938): 539–64.

Cohen, William. "Congressional Power to Validate Unconstitutional State Laws: A Forgotten Solution to an Old Engine." *Stanford Law Review* 35 (February 1983): 387–422.

Conlin, Timothy J., and Francois Vergniolle de Chantel. "The Rehnquist Court and Contemporary American Federalism." *Political Science Quarterly* 116 (2001): 753–75.

Cory, Dennis C., and Tauhidur Rahman. "Environmental Justice and Enforcement of the Safe Drinking Water Act: The Arizona Arsenic Experience," *Ecological Economic* 18 (April 15, 2009): 1825–837.

Corwin, Edward S. "National-State Cooperation—Its Present Possibilities." *Yale Law Journal* 46 (February 1937): 599–623.

———. "The Passing of Dual Federalism." *Virginia Law Review* 36 (February 1950): 1–24.

Crifield, Brevard, and H. Clyde Reeves. "Intergovernmental Relations: A View from the States." *Annals of the American Academy of Political and Social Science* 416 (November 1974): 99–107.

Daniels, Brigham, Erika Weinthal, and Blake Hudson. "Is an Exemption from US Groundwater Regulations a Loophole or a Noose? *Policy Sciences* 41 (September 2008): 205–20.

Davis, Charles E., Sandra K. Davis, and Denise Peacock. "State Implementation of the Surface Mining Control and Reclamation Act of 1977." *Policy Studies Review* (Autumn 1989): 109–19.

Davis, Mary J. "Unmasking the Presumption in Favor of Preemption." *South Carolina Law Review* 53 (Summer 2002): 967–1030.

Dernbach, John C. "Pennsylvania Implementation of the Surface Mining Control and Reclamation Act: An Assessment of How 'Cooperative Federalism' Can Make State Regulatory Programs More Effective." *University of Michigan Journal of Law Reform* 19 (Summer 1986): 903–67.

Diamond, Martin. "What the Framers Meant by Federalism." In Robert A. Goldman, ed., *A Nation of States: Essays on American Federalism*, 2nd ed. Chicago: Rand McNally College Publishing Company, 1974: 25–47.

Durham, G. Homer. "Politics and Administration in Intergovernmental Relations." *Annals of the American Academy of Political and Social Science* 207 (January 1940): 1–6.

Dwyer, John P. "The Role of State Law in an Era of Federal Preemption: Lessons from Environmental Regulation." *Law and Contemporary Problems* 60 (Summer 1997): 203–29.

Edgmon, Terry D., and Donald C. Menzel. "The Regulation of Coal Surface Mining in a Federal System." *Natural Resources Journal* 21 (April 1981): 245–65.

Fallon, Richard H., Jr. "Reflections on the Hart and Wechsler Paradigm," *Vanderbilt Law Review* 47 (May 1994): 953–87.

Farber, Daniel A. "Is the Supreme Court Irrelevant—Reflections on the Judicial Role in Environmental Law." *Minnesota Law Review* 81 (1997): 547–69.

———. "Taking Slippage Seriously: Noncompliance and Creative Compliance in Environmental Law." *Harvard Environmental Law Review* 23 (1999): 297–325.

———. "Triangulating the Future of Reinvention: Three Emerging Models of Environmental Protection." *University of Illinois Law Review* 2000, no. 1 (2000): 61–81.

Farside, Joseph A., Jr. "Atlantic States Marine Fishery Commission: Getting a Grip on Slippery Fisheries Management." *Roger Williams University Law Review* 11 (Fall 2005): 31–71.

Federsen, William F., Jr. "Turning the Tide on Water Quality." *Ecology Law Quarterly* 1 (1988): 69–102.

Fish, Jared. "*United States v. Robison*: The Case for Restoring Broad Jurisdictional Authority Under the Federal Clean Water Act in the Wake of Rapanos' Muddied Waters. *Ecology Law Quarterly* 36 (2009): 561–67.

Flatt, Victor P. "A Dirty River Runs Through It (The Failure of Enforcement in the Clean Water Act)." *Boston College Environmental Law Review* 25 (1997): 1–45.

Foley, Vincent J. "Deepwater Horizon: The Legal Fallout—The Framework for Liability, Fines, and Penalties for Oil Pollution." *Environmental Claims Journal* 22 (October–November 2010): 280–86.

Frankfurter, Felix, and James M. Landis. "The Compact Clause of the Constitution—A Study in Interstate Adjustments." *Yale Law Journal* 34 (May 1925): 685–758.

Freeman, Jody, and Daniel A. Farber. "Modular Environmental Regulation." *Duke Law Journal* 54 (February 2005): 795–912.

Gaffney, Brian P. "A Divided Duty: The Environmental Protection Agency's Dilemma." *Review of Litigation* (Spring 2007): 487–524.

Galloway, L. Thomas, and Tom Fitzgerald. "The Surface Mining Control and Reclamation Act of 1977: The Citizen's 'Act in the Hole.'" *Northern Kentucky Law Review* 8 (1981): 259–76.

Gardbaum, Stephen A. "The Nature of Preemption." *Cornell Law Review* 79 (1994): 767–815.

Garrett, Elizabeth. "States in a Federal System: Enhancing the Political Safeguards of Federalism? The Unfunded Mandates Reform Act of 1995." *Kansas Law Review* 45 (July 1997): 113–83.

Glickman, Robert L. "From Cooperative to Inoperative Federalism: The Perverse Mutation of Environmental Law and Policy." *Wake Forest Law Review* 41 (2006): 719–803.

Goodman, Frank, ed. "The Supreme Court's Federalism: Real or Imagined?" *Annals of the American Academy of Political and Social Science* 574 (March 2001): 9–194.

Graves, W. Brooke. "The Future of the American States." *American Political Science Review* 30 (February 1936): 24–50.

———. "State Constitutional Provisions for Federal-State Cooperation." *Annals of the American Academy of Political and Social Science* 18 (September 1935): 142–48.

Green, Edward M. "State and Federal Roles Under the Surface Mining Control and Reclamation Act of 1977." *Southern Illinois University Law Journal* 21 (1997): 531–51.

Green, Tristin K. "Complete Preemption: Removing the Mystery from Removal." *California Law Review* 86 (March 1998): 363–95.

Grout, Douglas E. "Interactions Between Striped Bass (Morone Saxatilis) Rebuilding Programmes and the Conservation of Atlantic Salmon (Salmo Salar) and Other Anadromous Fish Species in the USA." *ICES Journal of Marine Science* 63 (2006): 1346–352.

Hackney, Ryan. "Don't Mess with Houston, Texas: The Clean Air Act and State/Local Preemption." *Texas Law Review* 88 (2010): 639–68.

Harris, Joseph P. "The Future of Federal Grants-in-Aid." *Annals of the American Academy of Political and Social Science* 207 (January 1940): 14–26.

Hayes, Dion W. "Emasculating State Environmental Enforcement: The Supreme Court's Selective Adoption of the Preemption Doctrine." *William & Mary Environmental Law and Policy Review* 16, no. 1 (1991): 31–44.

Healy, Michael P. "Still Dirty Water After 25 Years: Water Quality Standard Enforcement and the Availability of Citizen Suits." *Ecology Law Quarterly* 24 (1997): 395–460.

Holcombe, Arthur N. "The Coercion of States in a Federal System." In Arthur MacMahon, ed., *Federalism: Mature and Emergent*. Garden City, NY: Doubleday and Company, 1955: 137–56.

Jaffe, Jill. "Scientific Uncertainty and the Regulation of Greenhouse Gases Under the Clean Air Act." *Ecology Law Quarterly* 37 (2010): 765–72.

Karkkainen, Bradley C. "Collaborative Ecosystem Governance: Scale, Complexity, and Dynamism." *Virginia Environmental Law Journal* 21 (2000–2001): 189–243.

Key, V. O. "State Legislation Facilitative of Federal Action." *Annals of the American Academy of Political and Social Science* 509 (January 1940): 7–13.

Kincaid, John, ed. "American Federalism: The Third Century." *Annals of the American Academy of Political and Social Science* 509 (May 1990): 1–152.

———. "From Cooperative to Coercive Federalism." In John Kincaid, ed., "American Federalism: The Third Century." *Annals of the American Academy of Political and Social Science* (May 1990): 139–52.

Koenig, Louis W. "Federal and State Cooperation Under the Constitution." *Michigan Law Review* 36 (March 1938): 752–85.

Konisky, David M. "Inequities in Enforcement?: Environmental Justice and Government Performance." *Journal of Policy Analysis and Management* 28, no. 1 (2009): 102–21.

Kurtz, Rick S. "Oil Pipeline Regulation, Culture, and Integrity: The 2006 BP North Slope Spill." *Public Integrity* 13, no. 1 (2011): 25–40.

Lantioin, Maris C. "Remedial Incentives for Enforcement of the Clean Air Act." *Ateneo Law Journal* 53 (March 2009): 936–51.

Laughlin, Tom. "Evaluating New Federalism Arguments in the Areas of the Environment: The Search for Empirical Measures." *NYU Environmental Law Journal* 13 (2005): 481–500.

Lawson, Gary, and Patricia B. Granger. "The 'Proper' Scope of Federal Power: A Jurisdictional Interpretation of the Sweeping Clause." *Duke Law Journal* 43 (November 1993): 267–336.

Leach, Richard H., ed. "Intergovernmental Relations in America Today." *Annals of the American Academy of Political and Social Science* 416 (May 1974):1–109.

———. "Intergovernmental Relations in the United States." *Annals of the American Academy of Political and Social Science* 416 (November 1974): 1–193.

Learner, Howard A. "Restraining Federal Preemption When There Is an 'Emerging Consensus' of State Environmental laws and Politics." *Northwestern University Law Review* 102, no. 2 (2008): 649–63.

Lee, Carol F. "The Political Safeguards of Federalism? Congressional Responses to Supreme Court Decisions on State and Local Liability." *Urban Lawyer* 20 (Spring 1988): 301–40.

MacManus, Susan A. "Mad About Mandates: The Issue of Who Should Pay for What Resurfaces." *Publius: The Journal of Federalism* 21 (Summer 2001): 59–75.

Mank, Bradford C. "The Murky Future of the Clean Water Act after *SWANCC*: Using a Hydrological Connection Approach to Saving the Clean Water Act." *Ecology Law Quarterly* 30 (2003): 811–91.

Marten, Bradley M. "Regulation of the Transportation of Hazardous Materials: A Critique and a Proposal." *Harvard Environmental Law Review* 5 (1981): 345–76.

McCoy, Charles F. "Federalism: The Lost Tradition." *Publius: The Journal of Federalism* 31 (Spring 2001): 1–14.

Meshkati, Najmedin. "Safety and Human Factors Considerations in Control Rooms of Oil and Gas Pipeline Systems: Conceptual Issues and Practical Observations." *International Journal of Occupational Safety and Ergonomics* 12, no. 1 (2006): 79–93.

McCarthy, Jack. "Manure Flow Raises Worry." *The Press Enterprise* (Riverside, California) (April 18, 1998): B3.

McCown, Brigham A., and Dawn W. Theiss. "Safeguarding the Energy Pipeline Transportation System & the Pipes Act of 2006." *Texas Journal of Oil, Gas, and Energy Law* 3, no. 1 (2008): 22–49.

Miller, Richard. "Implementing a Program of Cooperative Federalism in Surface Mining Policy." *Policy Studies Review* 9, no. 1 (1989): 79–87.

Moren, Harry. "The Difficulty of Fencing in Interstate Emissions: EPA's Clean Air Interstate Rule Fails to Make Good Neighbors." *Ecology Law Quarterly* 36 (2009): 525–52.

Moreno, Robert B. "Filling the Regulatory Gap: A Proposal for Restructuring the Clean Water Act's Two-Permit System." *Ecology Law Quarterly* 37 (2010): 285–316.

Nathan, Richard P. "The New Federalism Versus the Emerging New Structuralism." *Publius: The Journal of Federalism* 5 (Summer 1975): 111–29.

Nordhaus, Robert R., and Emily Pitlick. "Carbon Dioxide Pipeline Regulations." *Energy Law Journal* 30 (2009): 85–103.

Oates, Wallace E. "A Reconsideration of Environmental Federalism." Washington, DC: Resources for the Future, 2001.

O'Brien, David M. "The Rehnquist Court and Federal Preemption: In Search of a New Theory." *Publius: The Journal of Federalism* 23 (Fall 1993): 25–31

———. "The Supreme Court Intergovernmental Relations: What Happened to 'Our New Federalism'?" *Journal of Law and Politics* 9 (Summer 1993): 609–37.

Painter, Bill. "Dilution of a Solution." *The Environmental Forum* 3 (May/June 2007): 27–31.

Parker, Carol M. "The Pipeline Industry Meets Grief Unimaginable: Congress Reacts with the Pipeline Safety Improvement Act of 2002." *Natural Resources* 44 (Winter 2004): 243–82.

Pedersen, William F., Jr. "Turning the Tide on Water Quality." *Ecology Law Journal* 15, no. 1 (1988): 69–102.

Percival, Robert V. "Environmental Federalism: Historical Roots and Contemporary Models." *Maryland Law Review* 54 (1995): 1141–182.

Powell, H. Jefferson. "The Original Understanding of Original Intent." *Harvard Law Review* 98 (March 1985): 885–948.

"The Power of Congress to Subject Interstate Commerce to State Regulation." *University of Chicago Law Review* 3 (1935): 636–40.

Rafferty, Christopher. "Restoring Webster's Definition of 'Best' Under the Clean Air Act." *Ecology Law Quarterly* 37 (2010): 595–624.

Rahman, Tauhidur, et al. "Determinants of Environmental Noncompliance by Public Water Systems." *Contemporary Economic Policy* 28 (April 1010): 264–74.

"Randolph Board Sets Stricter Hog Standards.'" *Greensboro News & Record* (North Carolina) (March 24, 1998): B1.

"Recent Cases." *Harvard Law Review* 122 (2009): 982–89.

Reisenger, Will, Trenta A. Dougherty, and Nolan Moser. "Environmental Enforcement and Limits of Cooperative Federalism: Will Courts Allow Citizen Suits to Pick Up the Slack?" *Duke Environmental Law & Policy Forum* 10 (Winter 2010): 24–48.

Renz, Jeffrey T. "The Effect of Federal Legislation on the Historical State Powers of Pollution Control: Has Congress Muddied State Waters." *Montana Law Review* 43, no. 2 (2014): 1–20.

Revesz, Richard L. "Federalism and Environmental Regulation: A Public Choice Analysis." *Harvard Law Review* 115 (December 2001): 553–641.

———. "Federalism and Interstate Environmental Externalities." *University of Pennsylvania Law Review* 144 (June 1996): 2341–416.

Robinson, Heidi G. "If Your Grandfather Could Pollute, So Can Your Environmental 'Grandfather Clauses' and Their Role in Environmental Equity." *Catholic University Law Review* 45 (1995): 131–79.

Scheberle, Denise. "The Evolving Matrix of Environmental Federalism and Intergovernmental Relationships." *Publius: The Journal of Federalism* 35 (Winter 2005): 69–86.

Schechter, Mollie E. "The Surfacing Mining Control and Reclamation Act of 1977." *New York Law School Law Review* 4 (1980): 453–99.

Sciechitano, Michael J., and David M. Hedge. "From Coercion to Partnership in Federal Partial Preemption: SMCRA, RCRA, and OSHA Act." *Publius: The Journal of Federalism* 23 (Fall 1993): 107–21.

Seelye, Katharine Q. "U.S. Report Faults Efforts to Track Water Pollution," *New York Times* (March 27, 2003): 1, A19.

Seidenberg, Jennifer L. "Texas Independent Producers & Royalty Owners Association v. Environmental Protection Agency: Redefining the Role of Public Participation in the Clean Water Act." *Ecology Law Quarterly* 33 (2005): 699–724.

Shapiro, Robert A. "Toward a Theory of Interactive Federalism." *Iowa Law Review* 91 (2005): 243–317.

Steinbeck, Scott R., Richard B. Allen, and Eric Thunberg. "The Benefits of Rationalization: The Case of the American Lobster Fishery." *Marine Resource Economics* 23 (Spring 2008): 37–69.

Swanson, Katherine A. "The Cost of Doing Business: Corporate Vicarious Criminal Liability for the Negligent Discharge of Oil Under the Clean Water Act." *Washington Law Review* 84 (2009): 555–79.

Tietenberg, Tom. "Cap and Trade: Evolution of an Economic Idea." *Agriculture and Resource Economic Review* 39 (October 2010): 359–67.

Thompson, Walter. "The Trend Toward Federal Centralization." *Annals of the American Academy of Political and Social Science* 113 (1924): 172–82.

Van Putten, Mark C., and Bradley D. Jackson. "The Dilution of the Clean Water Act." *University of Michigan Journal of Law Reform* 2 (Summer 1986): 863–901.

Vestal, Theodore M. "Federal Administration of the Surface Mining Control and Reclamation Act of 1977 in Oklahoma." *Publius: the Journal of Federalism* 18 (Winter 1988): 45–60.

Wagner, James R. "Congress Clears Strip Mining Control Bill." *Congressional Quarterly Weekly* (July 23, 1977): 1495–500.

Wallick, Ruth. "GATT and Preemption of State and Local laws." *Government Finance Review* 10 (October 1994): 46–47.

Webber, Barbara S., and David J. Webber, "Promoting Economic Incentives for Environmental Protection in the Surface Mining Control and Reclamation Act of 1977: An Analysis of the Design and Implementation of Reclamation Performance Bonds." *Natural Resources Journal* 25 (April 1985): 389–414.

Wechsler, Herbert. "The Political Safeguards of Federalism: The Role of the States in the Composition and Selection of the National Government." *Columbia Law Review* 54 (1953): 543–60.

Williams, Douglas R. "Cooperative Federalism and the Clean Air Act: A Defense of Minimum Federal Standards." *Saint Louis University Public Law Review* 20 (2001): 67–120.

Williamson, Richard S. "The Self-Government Balancing Act: A View from the White House." *National Civic Review* 71 (January 1982): 19–22.

Yoo, John C. "The Judicial Safeguards of Federalism." *Southern California Law Review* 70 (July 1997): 1311–405.

Zimmerman, Joseph F. "Cities Versus Atoms." *National Civic Review* 60 (April 1961): 1–7.

———. "Congressional Preemption during the George W. Bush Administration." *Publius: The Journal of Federalism* 37 (Summer 2007): 432–52.

———. "Congressional Preemption: Removal of State Regulatory Powers." *PS: Political Science and Politics* 38 (July 2005): 375–79.

———. "Congressional Regulation of Subnational Governments." *PS: Political Science and Politics* 26 (June 1993): 177–81.

———. "Election Systems and Representative Democracy: Reflections on the Voting Rights Act of 1965." *National Civic Review* 84 (Fall 1995): 287–309.

———. "Federal Judicial Remedial Power: The Yonkers Case." *Publius: The Journal of Federalism* 20 (Summer 1990): 45–61.

———, ed. "Federal Preemption." *Publius: The Journal of Federalism* 23 (Fall 1993): 1–121.

———. "Federal Preemption Under Reagan's New Federalism." *Publius: The Journal of Federalism* 21 (Winter 1991): 7–28.

———. "The Federal Voting Rights Act and Alternative Election Systems." *William and Mary Law Review* 19 (Summer 1978): 621–60.

————. "Financing National Policy Through Mandates." *National Civic Review* 81 (Summer–Fall 1992): 367–73.

————. "National-State Relations: Cooperative Federalism in the Twentieth Century." *Publius: The Journal of Federalism* 31 (Spring 2001): 15–30.

————. "The Nature and Political Significance of Preemption." *PS: Political Science and Politics* 38 (July 2005): 359–62.

————. "The 104th Congress and Federalism." *Current Municipal Problems* 23, no. 4 (1997): 494–514.

————. "The Role of the State Legislature in Air Pollution Abatement." *Suffolk University Law Review* 5 (Spring 1971): 850–77.

————. "Overview of Voting Rights Laws" in *Communities & The Voting Rights Act*. Denver: National Civic League, 1996: 8–16.

————. "Preemption in the U.S. Federal System." *Publius: The Journal of Federalism* 23 (Fall 1993): 1–13.

————. "Regulating Intergovernmental Relations in the 1990s." *Annals of the American Academy of Political and Social Science* 509 (May 1990): 48–72.

————. "Relieving the Fiscal Burdens of State and Federal Mandates and Restraints." *Current Municipal Problems* 19, no. 2 (1992): 2165–224.

————. "Trends in Congressional Preemption." *The Book of the States 2003*. Lexington, KY: The Council of State Governments, 2003: 32–37.

————. "Zoning for Atomic Energy Uses," *Zoning Digest* 16 (1964): 161–69.

UNPUBLISHED MATERIAL

Crotty, Patricia M. "The New Federalism Game: Options for the States." Paper presented at the annual meeting of the Northeastern Political Science Association, Philadelphia, November 14–16, 1985.

Index

Abandoned Shipwreck Act of
1987, 79
Adler, Robert S., 22
administrative agency preemption,
19
administrative regulatory structure,
21–23
Advisory Commission on
Intergovernmental Relations,
26, 108–09
Air Quality Act of 1967, 55–56,
109–10
Airline Deregulation Act of 1978,
106–07
air-quality standards preemption,
53–66
alternatives to interstate suits,
61–63
Americans with Disabilities Act of
1990, 103
Articles of Confederation, 3–5
Atlantic Striped Bass Conservation
Act, 78–79, 96–97
at-large voting system, 87
authorization of state lawsuits,
73–75

Black, Hugo, 14
Brutus, 9–10
Burger, Warren, 90

Buzbee, William W., 65

Capital Markets Efficiency Act of
1996, 74
Children Online Privacy Protection
Act of 1998, 75
Clark, Jane Perry, 101–02
Clean Air Act Amendments of
1970, 56–57, 63, 66
accomplishments, 64–66
Sierra Club v. Ruckelshaus, 58
Clean Air Act Amendments of
1977, 58–59
Clean Air Act Amendments of
1990, 59–60
Clean Water Act, 41–45
Clinton, George, 92
Coast Guard Authorization Act of
1984, 78
Coastal Zone Management Act of
1972, 77–78
Commission on Intergovernmental
Relations, 23–26
congressional preemption, 15–19
constitutional convention, 5–7
constitutional developments, 3–28
Consumer Credit Reporting Reform
Act of 1996, 74–75
Consumer Product Safety
Improvement Act of 1990, 74

contingent preemption statutes, 83–99

Controlling the Assault of Non-Solicited Pornography and Marketing Act of 2003, 75

cooperative enforcement, 71–75

court interpretation, 63–64

delegated powers, 11–12

Eisenhower, Dwight, 23–24

Elazar, Daniel J., 104

Electronic Signatures in Global and National Commerce Act of 2000, 79

Energy Policy Act of 2008, 98

expansion of national powers, 23–27

export of pollutants, 62–63

Federal Environmental Pesticide Control Act of 1972, 74

federal financial assistance to states, 30–31

federal legal voting standards of nondiscrimination, 91–95

federal maximum standards, 67–71

Federalist and Antifederalist papers, 8–10

Federalist No. 39, 44, and 45, 9

Fifteenth Amendment, 84

Frankfurter, Felix, 62, 80–81, 105–06

general water quality, 31–38

general welfare clause, 14–15

Giovinazzo, Christopher T., 65

Glickman, Robert L., 110

grain inspection, 72

Gramm-Leach-Bliley Financial Modernization Act of 1999, 67–71, 97–98

Greenstone, Michael, 65

Hamilton, Alexander, 8–9, 12, 101

Hare, Thomas, 93

Hasidic Jews, 88–91, 96

hazardous and solid waste, 73

Hotel and Motel Fire Safety Act of 1990, 79

Hyde, Albert C., 58

Imperium in Imperio, 1

implied powers, 12–13

innovative statutes, 77–80, 106–10

interstate compacts, 105–06

Jackson, Lisa P., 65–66

Jefferson, Thomas, 12, 23

Johnson Act of 1951, 77

Jones, Charles O., 53–54

Junk Fax Prevention Act of 2005, 75

Konisky, David M., 56, 62

Krupnick, Alan, 65

Landis, James M., 80–81, 105–06

limited nomination and voting, 92–93

Low-Level Atomic Energy Act, 72

Madison, James, 8–9, 83–84

McCarran-Ferguson of 1945, 67

minimum national standards preemption, 29–51, 107–10
Moren, Harry, 60
Morgenstern, Richard, 65
motor vehicle pollution control act of 1965, 54–55

national association of insurance commissioners, 97
nature of preemption, 1–28
enactment pace, 18–19
significance, 19–21
nuclear waste policy act of 1982, 78
Nutrition Labeling and Education Act of 1920, 74

Oil Pollution Act of 1990, 74
Omnibus Consolidated Appropriations Act for Fiscal Year 1996, 75
Oren, Craig N., 66
Ozone Transport Commission, 59–60

Pataki, George E., 61
Port and Tanker Safety Act of 1978, 78

railroad inspection, 72
Reagan, Ronald, 26
recommendations, 80–81
regional greenhouse initiative, 61
regulatory authority turn-backs, 71–75
reserved powers, 2
Restore Online Shoppers Confidence Act of 2010, 75
resultant powers, 13

Riegle-Neal Interstate Banking and Branching Efficiency Act of 1994, 79
Roberts, John, 96

Safe Drinking Water Act, 45–50
single-transferable vote form of proportional representation, 93–95
Social Security Act of 1935, 31
supremacy of the law clause, 13–14
Surface Mining and Reclamation Act, 38–41

Telemarketing and Consumer Fraud and Abuse Prevention Act of 1994, 74
Telephone Consumer Protection Act of 1991, 74
Telephone Disclosure and Dispute Resolution Act of 1992, 74
Tietenberg, Tom, 65
Toxic Substances Control Act of 1976, 78
Twenty-First Amendment Enforcement Act of 2000, 75

United Jewish Organization, Incorporated v. Wilson, 89–91
U.S. Advisory Commission on Intergovernmental Relations, 108–09
U.S. Government Accountability Office, 55–56

Vile, J.C., 101
Voting Rights Act of 1965, 84–86, 91, 98

Water Quality Act of 1965, 29, 55–56, 77, 107–09

Whitman v. American Trucking Associations, 63–64

Williams, Douglas R., 66

Williamson Richard S., 27

Woods, Neal D., 56, 62

Yates, Robert, 9

Zorn, Grahma, 59

www.ingramcontent.com/pod-product-compliance
Lightning Source LLC
Chambersburg PA
CBHW030335270326
41926CB00010B/1630